The ultimate Zojirushi BREAD MACHINE Cookbook

Wholesome Recipes for Every Occasion with Your Zojirushi Bread Machine

Jorge V. Kautz

TABLE OF CONTENT

INTRODUCTION

Zojirushi Bread Machine Cookbook: The Ultimate! No matter your baking experience, this handbook will help you make great handmade bread easily.

Bread baking at home is now easier and more convenient, thanks to the Zojirushi bread maker. You can make everything from white loaves to gourmet sourdoughs in your kitchen with its diverse features and exact settings.

Our Zojirushi bread machine cookbook has delicious recipes. From classics to originals, each dish is meticulously prepared for exceptional flavor and texture.

This book has recipes for everything from robust sandwich bread for breakfast to sweet treats for dessert to savory loaves for dinner. Even beginners may confidently obtain bakery-quality results with step-by-step instructions and practical recommendations.

Refresh your Zojirushi bread machine, roll up your sleeves, and prepare to bake excellent bread. It's infinite, and the smell of fresh bread will brighten your kitchen. Nice baking!

ABOUT THE ULTIMATE ZOJIRUSHI BREAD MACHINE

Diverse Recipe Collection: This cookbook offers a wide range of bread varieties to satisfy every taste, from traditional white bread and whole wheat to specialty breads like cinnamon raisin and sourdough.

Creative Variations: Unleash your imagination in the kitchen with these creative recipes for sweet bread, artisan loaves, gluten-free bread, and even pizza dough.

Step-by-Step Instructions: With the simple, uncomplicated directions provided with each recipe, even inexperienced users can use a Zojirushi bread maker to produce delectable results.

Tips and Tricks: Find out useful hints and techniques for optimizing flavor and texture and fixing typical problems with your Zojirushi bread maker.

Nutritional Information: Nutritious information is included in many recipes, so you may make educated diet decisions and enjoy homemade bread guilt-free.

TIPS AND TRICKS FOR MAKING BREAD

Measure Ingredients Precisely: Making bread is a science, and precise measures are essential. When feasible, weigh wheat and liquids using a kitchen scale.

Use Fresh Ingredients: The greatest results will come from using fresh yeast, wheat, and other components. Verify the expiration dates on your yeast and flour to ensure freshness.

Follow the Recipe: Follow the recipe exactly until you're comfortable experimenting with changes, especially if you're new to cooking bread.

Adjust Liquid Levels: You may need to change your recipe's liquid amount due to humidity, flour type, and altitude. The kneading dough should create a smooth, elastic ball.

Room Temperature Ingredients: Keep components, especially liquids like water and milk, at room temperature. Cold substances delay yeast activation.

Test Your Yeast: If yeast isn't fresh, prove it before using. Sprinkle yeast over a teaspoon of sugar in warm water (110-115°F) and let it froth. Not foaming after 5-10 minutes may indicate inactivity.

Experiment with Flours: Bread, all-purpose, and whole wheat flours have varied textures and tastes. To discover your favorite combination, experiment.

Use the Right Yeast: Many bread machine recipes ask for instant or bread machine yeast. These are meant to be blended with dry ingredients without proof.

Add Ingredients in the Right Order: According to your bread machine handbook, add ingredients in order. In a flour well, liquids go in first, dry ingredients follow, and yeast goes last.

Don't Overdo It: Avoid overworking your breadmaker. Check your machine's capacity and obey flour and liquid limits.

Monitor the Dough: Check the dough occasionally while kneading. The ball should be smooth and elastic. Add water a teaspoon at a time if dry. Add flour tablespoons at a time if it is too moist.

Customize: Once you're acquainted with basic recipes, try adding nuts, seeds, dried fruits, herbs, and spices to customize your bread.

Never forget that practice makes perfect! If the first few loaves aren't flawless, don't give up. You'll gain experience and confidence in your bread-making abilities with practice and patience.

CLASSIC WHITE BREAD

Total Time: 3 hours 40 minutes | Prep Time: 10 minutes

Ingredients:

1 cup warm water	2 tablespoons white sugar
2 1/4 teaspoons active dry yeast	1/4 cup vegetable oil
3 cups bread flour	1 1/2 teaspoons salt

Directions:

(1) The bread machine pan has to be filled with warm water, sugar, and yeast. Let it rest for five to ten minutes or until frothy. *(2)* Make sure the pan has oil, flour, and salt in it. *(3)* Begin the cycle on your bread maker after selecting the Basic/White Bread setting from the selection menu. *(4)* Remove the bread from the machine as soon as the cycle is finished, and let it cool on a wire rack before slicing.

WHOLE WHEAT HONEY OAT BREAD

Total Time: 3 hours 45 minutes | Prep Time: 15 minutes

Ingredients:

1 1/4 cups warm water	3 tablespoons honey
2 tablespoons vegetable oil	1 1/2 cups whole wheat flour
1 cup bread flour	1/2 cup rolled oats
1 1/2 teaspoons salt	2 1/4 teaspoons active dry yeast

Directions:

(1) The pan of the bread machine should be filled with warm water, honey, and oil. *(2)* Add the whole wheat flour, bread flour, oats, and salt to the batter in addition to the yeast. Start the cycle on your bread machine after selecting the Whole Wheat setting from the several options. *(3)* Remove the bread from the machine as soon as the cycle is finished, and let it cool on a wire rack before slicing.

ITALIAN CIABATTA

Total Time: 4 hours | Prep Time: 20 minutes

Ingredients:

1 1/2 cups warm water	2 tablespoons olive oil
3 cups bread flour	1 1/2 teaspoons salt
1 1/2 teaspoons active dry yeast	

Directions:

(1) Fill the bread machine pan with warm water and olive oil. *(2)* Season with salt, yeast, and bread flour. *(3)* Put your bread maker on Dough mode and begin the cycle. *(4)* Take the Dough out of the machine after the dough cycle is finished, then form it into two ciabatta loaves. *(5)* After putting the loaves on a parchment paper-lined baking pan, give them 30 to 40 minutes to rise. *(6)* Adjust oven temperature to 425°F (220°C). *(7)* The ciabatta loaves should be baked for 20 to 25 minutes or until golden brown. *(8)* Take them out of the oven and let cool on a wire rack before serving.

CINNAMON SWIRL BREAD

Total Time: 3 hours 45 minutes | Prep Time: 15 minutes

Ingredients:

1 cup warm milk (110°F/45°C)	1 egg
3 tablespoons butter, softened	3 cups bread flour
1/4 cup white sugar	1 1/2 teaspoons salt
2 1/4 teaspoons active dry yeast	2 tablespoons ground cinnamon
1/4 cup brown sugar	

Directions:

(1) To the bread machine pan, add butter, egg, and heated milk. *(2)* Sprinkle with yeast, white sugar, bread flour, and salt. *(3)* On your bread machine, select the Dough setting and begin the cycle. *(4)* Take the Dough out of the machine and roll it into a rectangle after the dough cycle is finished. *(5)* Combine the powdered cinnamon and brown sugar, then evenly distribute it over the Dough. *(6)* Form the Dough into a log and put it in a loaf pan that has been oiled. *(7)* For thirty to forty minutes, let the pan rise, covered with a cloth. *(8)* Set the oven's temperature to 175°C/350°F. *(9)* For thirty to thirty-five minutes, or until golden brown, bake the cinnamon swirl bread. *(10)* Take it out of the oven and allow it to cool down on a cooling rack before slicing.

CHOCOLATE CHIP BANANA BREAD

Total Time: 3 hours 45 minutes | Prep Time: 15 minutes

Ingredients:

3 ripe bananas, mashed	1/2 cup white sugar
1/2 cup brown sugar	1/2 cup vegetable oil
2 eggs	2 cups all-purpose flour
1 teaspoon baking soda	1/2 teaspoon salt
1 cup chocolate chips	

Directions:

(1) Mashed bananas, white sugar, brown sugar, vegetable oil, and eggs should all be thoroughly mixed in a big basin. *(2)* Stir the baking soda, salt, and all-purpose flour into the banana mixture just until incorporated. *(3)* Add chocolate chips and fold. *(4)* Transfer the mixture to the pan of the bread maker. *(5)* On your bread maker, select the Quick Bread preset and begin the cycle. *(6)* Before slicing the bread, remove it from the machine once the cycle is complete and set it on a wire rack to cool.

BASIL AND SUN-DRIED TOMATO BREAD

Total Time: 3 hours | Prep Time: 15 minutes

Ingredients:

1 cup water	3 tablespoons olive oil
3 cups bread flour	2 tablespoons sugar
1 1/2 teaspoons salt	2 teaspoons active dry yeast
1/2 cup chopped sun-dried tomatoes (packed in oil)	1/4 cup chopped fresh basil leaves
1/4 cup grated Parmesan cheese	

Directions:

(1) In the bread machine pan, combine water, olive oil, bread flour, sugar, salt, and yeast according to the manufacturer's instructions. Pick the dough cycle and start. *(2)* Place the Dough on a lightly floured board after removing it from the machine. *(3)* Stir in the chopped sun-dried tomatoes, basil leaves, and Parmesan cheese until equally distributed. *(4)* Make a loaf and put it in a buttered pan. *(5)* After an hour in a warm place, wrapped with a fresh kitchen towel, it should have doubled in size. *(6)* Heat oven to 375°F (190°C). *(7)* Bake the bread at 190°F (88°C) for 25 to 30 minutes or until golden brown. Allow the pan to cool for ten minutes before moving it to a wire rack to complete the cooling process.

PESTO PARMESAN BREAD

Total Time: 3 hours 30 minutes | Prep Time: 20 minutes

Ingredients:

1 cup water	3 tablespoons olive oil
3 cups bread flour	2 tablespoons pesto sauce
1 1/2 teaspoons salt	2 teaspoons active dry yeast
1/4 cup grated Parmesan cheese	

Directions:

(1) Following the manufacturer's directions, mix water, olive oil, bread flour, pesto sauce, salt, and yeast in the bread machine pan. *(2)* Start the dough cycle. *(3)* Move the Dough from the machine to a lightly floured board. *(4)* Stir in the grated Parmesan cheese gently. *(5)* Fill a loaf pan with oil and add the Dough. *(6)* Once it has doubled in size, cover it with a fresh kitchen towel and let it rise in a warm place for one hour and thirty minutes. Heat the oven to 190°C. Bake until golden brown and 190°F (88°C) inside, 30–35 minutes. *(7)* After ten minutes in the pan, transfer it to a wire rack to cool completely.

CRANBERRY WALNUT BREAD

Total Time: 3 hours 45 minutes | Prep Time: 25 minutes

Ingredients:

1 cup water	3 tablespoons olive oil
3 cups bread flour	2 tablespoons sugar
1 1/2 teaspoons salt	2 teaspoons active dry yeast
1/2 cup dried cranberries	1/2 cup chopped walnuts

Directions:

(1) In the bread machine pan, combine water, olive oil, bread flour, sugar, salt, and yeast according to the manufacturer's instructions. Pick the dough cycle and start. **(2)** Place the Dough on a lightly floured board after removing it from the machine. **(3)** Add dried cranberries and chopped walnuts and mix gently. **(4)** Make a loaf and put it in a buttered pan. **(5)** Cover with a fresh kitchen towel and let rise for two hours in a warm place to double in size. Heat oven to 375°F (190°C). **(6)** Golden brown and 190°F (88°C) are the goals of 35-40 minutes of baking. **(7)** Allow the pan to cool for ten minutes before moving it to a wire rack to complete the cooling process.

APPLE CINNAMON BREAD

Total Time: 4 hours | Prep Time: 30 minutes

Ingredients:

1 cup water	3 tablespoons olive oil
3 cups bread flour	2 tablespoons sugar
1 1/2 teaspoons salt	2 teaspoons active dry yeast
1 cup peeled and diced apples	1 tablespoon ground cinnamon

Directions:

(1) In the bread machine pan, combine water, olive oil, bread flour, sugar, salt, and yeast according to the manufacturer's instructions. Pick the dough cycle and start. **(2)** Place the Dough on a lightly floured board after removing it from the machine. **(3)** Gently mix in diced apples and ground cinnamon. **(4)** Make a loaf and put it in a buttered pan. **(5)** It should double in size after 2 hours and 30 minutes in a warm environment covered with a clean kitchen towel. **(6)** Heat oven to 375°F (190°C). **(7)** Bake the bread at 190°F (88°C) for 40 to 45 minutes or until golden brown. **(8)** Allow the pan to cool for ten minutes before moving it to a wire rack to complete the cooling process.

LEMON POPPY SEED BREAD

Total Time: 3 hours 15 minutes | Prep Time: 10 minutes

Ingredients:

1 cup water	3 tablespoons olive oil
3 cups bread flour	2 tablespoons sugar
1 1/2 teaspoons salt	2 teaspoons active dry yeast
Zest of 2 lemons	2 tablespoons poppy seeds

Directions:

(1) In the bread machine pan, combine water, olive oil, bread flour, sugar, salt, and yeast according to the manufacturer's instructions. Pick the dough cycle and start. **(2)** Place the Dough on a lightly floured board after removing it from the machine. **(3)** Gently mix in lemon zest and poppy seeds. **(4)** Make a loaf and put it in a buttered pan. **(5)** Let it rise in a warm place for one hour and fifteen minutes, covered with a fresh kitchen towel, or until it has doubled in size. **(6)** Preheat oven to 190°C/375°F. **(7)** Bake for 25 to 30 minutes, or until the bread is 190°F (88°C) and golden brown. **(8)** Allow the pan to cool for ten minutes before moving it to a wire rack to complete the cooling process.

GARLIC HERB BREADSTICKS

Total Time: 2 hours | Prep Time: 20 minutes

Ingredients:

1 cup warm water	2 tablespoons olive oil
3 cups bread flour	2 tablespoons sugar
1 teaspoon salt	2 teaspoons active dry yeast
2 tablespoons dried herbs (such as rosemary, thyme, and oregano)	2 cloves garlic, minced
1/4 cup grated Parmesan cheese	Additional olive oil for brushing

Directions:

(1) Put olive oil and warm water in the bread machine pan. **(2)** As directed by the maker, add the yeast, sugar, salt, and bread flour to the pan in that order. **(3)** After choosing Dough, turn on the machine. **(4)** Take it out of the machine after the dough cycle and split it into twelve equal halves. **(5)** Place each section on a baking sheet that has been preheated and roll it into a rope. **(6)** Under a fresh kitchen towel, allow the Dough to rise for half an hour in a warm place. **(7)** Heat the oven to 190°C. **(8)** Mix dry herbs, minced garlic, and grated Parmesan in a small bowl. *(9)* Spread olive oil on rising breadsticks and sprinkle herb mixture. *(10)* Bake breadsticks for 15-20 minutes till golden brown. *(11)* Serve hot and enjoy!

EVERYTHING BAGEL BREAD

Total Time: 3 hours | Prep Time: 25 minutes

Ingredients:

1 1/4 cups warm water (110°F/45°C)	2 tablespoons olive oil
3 cups bread flour	2 tablespoons sugar
1 1/2 teaspoons salt	2 teaspoons active dry yeast
3 tablespoons everything bagel seasoning	

Directions:

(1) Pour the heated water and olive oil into the bread maker pan. *(2)* As directed by the maker, add the yeast, sugar, salt, and bread flour to the pan in that order. *(3)* After choosing Dough, turn on the machine. *(4)* After taking the Dough out of the machine, shape it into a loaf. *(5)* With an oiled loaf pan and a clean kitchen towel over the Dough, it won't double in size. Allow it to rest for half an hour to an hour. *(6)* Preheat oven to 190°C. *(7)* Sprinkle the everything bagel seasoning evenly over the bread that has risen. *(8)* Bake for 25 to 30 minutes, or until the bread is hollow when tapped and has a golden brown color. *(9)* Before moving the bread onto a wire rack, let it cool in the pan for ten minutes. *(10)* Cut and serve as desired.

HAWAIIAN SWEET BREAD

Total Time: 3 hours 30 minutes | Prep Time: 30 minutes

Ingredients:

1/2 cup pineapple juice	1/4 cup milk
2 tablespoons unsalted butter	1 egg
3 cups bread flour	1/4 cup sugar
1 teaspoon salt	2 teaspoons active dry yeast
1/2 cup dried pineapple, chopped	1/4 cup shredded coconut (optional)

Directions:

(1) Melt butter, pineapple juice, and milk in a small pot. Mildly cold. *(2)* Add beaten egg to the cooled mixture. *(3)* Bread machine pan with ingredients. *(4)* The manufacturer recommends adding bread flour, sugar, salt, and yeast to the pan in order. *(5)* Select Dough and start. *(6)* Add dried pineapple and shredded coconut (if used) and knead for a few minutes after the dough cycle. *(7)* Take the Dough out of the machine and make a round loaf. *(8)* Once the Dough has been allowed to rest in a warm location for fifteen minutes while being covered with a clean kitchen cloth, its volume will have doubled. *(9)* To prepare the cake, grease a circular pan with vegetable oil. *(10)* Preheat oven to 350°F (175°C). *(11)* Bake until bread is golden brown and hollow when tapped, 25–30 minutes. *(12)* After the bread cools in the pan for ten minutes, transfer it to a wire rack. *(13)* Slice, serve.

GLUTEN-FREE WHITE BREAD

Total Time: 3 hours 10 minutes | Prep Time: 10 minutes | Yields: 1 loaf

Ingredients:

1 1/2 cups warm water (110°F)	2 tablespoons honey
2 large eggs	1/4 cup olive oil
3 cups gluten-free all-purpose flour	1/4 cup almond flour
1/4 cup potato starch	1/4 cup tapioca flour
1 1/2 teaspoons xanthan gum	1 teaspoon salt
2 1/4 teaspoons active dry yeast	

Directions:

(1) To make bread, put olive oil, eggs, honey, and warm water into the bread pan of your Zojirushi bread maker. *(2)* Combine the almond flour, potato starch, tapioca flour, xanthan gum, salt, yeast, and gluten-free all-purpose flour in a separate basin. Whisk to combine. *(3)* To make bread, combine the dry ingredients with the wet ones in the pan in the specified sequence as directed by the manufacturer. *(4)* Turn on your bread machine to the "Gluten-Free" cycle. *(5)* Carefully take the bread pan out of the machine

when the cycle ends before slicing. Transfer the pan to a cooling rack made of wire.

GLUTEN-FREE SEEDED BREAD

Total Time: 3 hours 45 minutes | Prep Time: 20 minutes | Yields: 1 loaf

Ingredients:

1 1/4 cups warm water (110°F)	2 tablespoons honey
2 large eggs	1/4 cup olive oil
2 1/4 cups gluten-free all-purpose flour	1/4 cup almond flour
1/4 cup ground flaxseed	1/4 cup sunflower seeds
1/4 cup pumpkin seeds	1 1/2 teaspoons xanthan gum
1 teaspoon salt	2 1/4 teaspoons active dry yeast

Directions:

(1) Melt the honey, eggs, and olive oil in the bread pan of your Zojirushi bread maker. *(2)* A second bowl should be used to whisk together the following Ingredients: almond flour, gluten-free all-purpose flour, ground flaxseed, sunflower seeds, pumpkin seeds, xanthan gum, salt, and yeast. *(3)* Following the manufacturer-recommended order, combine the dry ingredients with the wet ones in the bread pan. *(4)* Before beginning the cycle, make sure your bread machine is set to the "Gluten-Free" option. *(5)* Before slicing, carefully remove the bread pan from the machine when the cycle stops and set it on a wire rack to cool.

GLUTEN-FREE BANANA NUT BREAD

Total Time: 3 hours | Prep Time: 15 minutes

Ingredients:

2 ripe bananas, mashed	3 eggs
1/4 cup melted coconut oil	1/4 cup honey
1 teaspoon vanilla extract	2 cups gluten-free flour blend
1 teaspoon baking powder	1/2 teaspoon baking soda
1/2 teaspoon salt	1/2 cup chopped walnuts

Directions:

(1) Your Zojirushi bread maker needs to be preheated. *(2)* Mix the mashed bananas, eggs, honey, melted coconut oil, and vanilla extract in a big bowl and whisk to mix. *(3)* Combine the salt, baking soda, gluten-free flour blend, and baking powder in a separate basin. *(4)* While whisking constantly, slowly incorporate the dry ingredients into the wet mixture. Mix gently to avoid clumping. *(5)* Combine with the chopped walnuts. *(6)* Transfer the batter to the Zojirushi bread machine's pan. *(7)* Press the start button after selecting the gluten-free option. *(8)* Before cutting and serving, carefully transfer the banana nut bread from the baking sheet to a wire rack to cool when the baking cycle is finished.

GLUTEN-FREE CINNAMON RAISIN BREAD

Total Time: 3 hours 30 minutes | Prep Time: 20 minutes

Ingredients:

1 1/2 cups warm water	2 tablespoons honey
2 tablespoons melted butter	3 cups gluten-free flour blend
1 teaspoon salt	1 1/2 teaspoons ground cinnamon
1/2 cup raisins	2 1/4 teaspoons active dry yeast

Directions:

(1) To make bread in your Zojirushi bread machine, combine warm water, honey, and melted butter in the pan. *(2)* In another bowl, combine the gluten-free flour mix, salt, and cinnamon powder. Whisk to combine. *(3)* Arrange the dry ingredients in a layer on top of the wet ones in the bread pan. *(4)* On top of the dry ingredients, evenly distribute the raisins. *(5)* Toss the active dry yeast into the dry ingredients after making a little well in the middle. *(6)* Turn your bread maker to the gluten-free setting and hit the start button. *(7)* Before cutting and serving, carefully take the cinnamon raisin bread from the pan once the baking cycle is finished. Allow to cool on a wire rack.

GLUTEN-FREE PIZZA DOUGH

Total Time: 2 hours 30 minutes | Prep Time: 10 minutes

Ingredients:

1 cup warm water	2 tablespoons olive oil
2 1/2 cups gluten-free flour blend	1 teaspoon salt
1 teaspoon sugar	2 1/4 teaspoons active dry yeast

Directions:

(1) Pour warm water and olive oil into the bread pan of your Zojirushi bread machine. *(2)* The gluten-free flour mix, sugar, and salt should be mixed in a different bowl. *(3)* Arrange the dry ingredients in a layer on top of the wet ones in the bread pan. *(4)* Toss the active dry yeast into the dry ingredients after making a little well in the middle. *(5)* Just press the start button after selecting the pizza dough option on your bread machine. *(6)* After the dough cycle finishes, take the Dough out of the bread pan and lightly flour the surface. Roll it out until it reaches the thickness you desire. *(7)* Before baking, top with your preferred toppings and follow the directions on your pizza recipe.

LOW-CARB ALMOND FLOUR BREAD

Total Time: 3 hours 15 minutes | Prep Time: 15 minutes

Ingredients:

1 cup almond flour	1/4 cup coconut flour
1/4 cup ground flaxseed	1/4 cup psyllium husk powder
1 teaspoon baking powder	1/2 teaspoon salt
4 eggs	1/4 cup melted butter
1/4 cup unsweetened almond milk	

Directions:

(1) Your Zojirushi bread maker needs to be preheated. *(2)* The flours of almonds, coconuts, ground flaxseed, psyllium husk, baking soda, and salt should be mixed in a big basin. *(3)* Combine the almond milk, melted butter, and eggs in another bowl and whisk until smooth. *(4)* Gradually stir in the liquid components slowly and steadily until a dough forms. Fill the bread pan of your Zojirushi bread machine with the

Dough. *(5)* Choose the low-carb option and hit the start button. *(6)* The almond flour bread should be removed from the pan with care once the baking cycle is finished. After cooling on a wire rack, it can be served or sliced.

LOW-SODIUM BREAD

Total Time: 3 hours 30 minutes | Prep Time: 20 minutes

Ingredients:

1 1/2 cups warm water	2 tablespoons olive oil
3 cups bread flour	1 1/2 teaspoons salt
1 1/2 teaspoons sugar	2 1/4 teaspoons active dry yeast

Directions:

(1) The bread pan of your Zojirushi bread maker should be filled with olive oil and warm water. *(2)* In still another bowl, whisk together the bread flour, sugar, and salt. Arrange the dry ingredients in a layer on top of the wet ones in the bread pan. *(3)* Toss the active dry yeast into the dry ingredients after making a little well in the middle. *(4)* Before starting your bread machine, make sure it is set to the low-sodium option. *(5)* Before cutting and serving, carefully remove the low-sodium bread from the bread pan once the baking cycle is finished. Allow to cool on a wire rack.

LOW-FAT SANDWICH BREAD

Total Time: 3 hours 30 minutes | Prep Time: 15 minutes | Yield: 1 loaf

Ingredients:

1 cup water, room temperature	2 tablespoons honey
2 tablespoons olive oil	3 cups bread flour
1/4 cup nonfat dry milk	1 1/2 teaspoons salt
2 1/4 teaspoons active dry yeast	

Directions:

(1) Please place the ingredients into the pan of the bread machine in the order that they are listed. *(2)* When using your Zojirushi bread machine, choose the "Basic" or "White Bread" mode, and then select the crust color that you

want to use. *(3)* To begin making bread, just push the machine's start button. *(4)* Slice the bread once it has cooled for 30 minutes on a wire rack after baking.

HIGH-PROTEIN BREAD

Total Time: 3 hours 45 minutes | Prep Time: 20 minutes | Yield: 1 loaf

Ingredients:

1 1/4 cups warm water (110°F)	3 tablespoons honey
2 tablespoons olive oil	3 cups bread flour
1/4 cup vital wheat gluten	2 teaspoons salt
2 1/4 teaspoons active dry yeast	

Directions:

(1) The pan for the bread machine should be filled with warm water and honey. Stir it to dissolve the honey. *(2)* In the sequence that is mentioned, add the yeast, pepper, bread flour, vital wheat gluten, and olive oil to the pan. *(3)* While using your Zojirushi bread maker, choose the "Wheat" or "Whole Wheat" preset, as well as the color of the crust you want to use. *(4)* Once you have pressed the start button, the bread machine will begin to knead, rise, and bake the Dough. Remove the loaf from the pan with care once it is finished cooking, and then place it on a wire rack to cool.

SEEDED WHOLE GRAIN BREAD

Total Time: 4 hours | Prep Time: 25 minutes | Yield: 1 loaf

Ingredients:

1 1/4 cups warm water (110°F)	2 tablespoons honey
2 tablespoons olive oil	2 cups whole wheat flour
1 cup bread flour	1/4 cup mixed seeds (such as sesame seeds, sunflower seeds, and flaxseeds)
2 tablespoons wheat germ	1 1/2 teaspoons salt
2 1/4 teaspoons active dry yeast	

Directions:

(1) The honey and warm water should be mixed together in the pan of the bread machine. The honey should be dissolved by stirring. *(2)* The following ingredients should be added to the pan in the order that they are listed: olive oil, whole wheat flour, bread flour, mixed seeds, wheat germ, salt, and yeast. *(3)* Make sure that your Zojirushi bread machine is set to the "Whole Wheat" or "Multi-Grain" preset, and then choose the crust color that you want. *(4)* The bread machine will start the dough-making process (mixing, kneading, rising, and baking) as soon as you push the start button. After the loaf is done cooking, take it out of the pan and set it on a wire rack to cool.

RUSTIC ARTISAN LOAF

Total Time: 5 hours 30 minutes | Prep Time: 30 minutes | Yield: 1 loaf

Ingredients:

1 1/2 cups warm water (110°F)	1 tablespoon honey
2 tablespoons olive oil	3 1/2 cups bread flour
2 teaspoons salt	2 1/4 teaspoons active dry yeast

Directions:

(1) Stir warm water and honey in the bread machine pan until dissolved. *(2)* In sequence, add olive oil, bread flour, salt, and yeast to the pan. *(3)* Turn on your Zojirushi bread maker to the "Dough" cycle and press the start button. The Dough has to be mixed and kneaded by the machine. Remove the Dough from the machine and form it into a rustic loaf on a floured board. *(4)* Evenly distribute the Dough onto a parchment-lined baking sheet. It will have grown in size by half an hour after rising in a warm spot loosely wrapped with plastic. *(5)* Heat the oven to 200°C. Remove the risen loaf's plastic wrap and slit the top with a sharp knife. *(6)* The bread should be golden brown and hollow when tapped after 25–30 minutes in the preheated oven. *(7)* Slice and serve the loaf after cooling on a wire rack.

SPINACH AND FETA BREAD

Total Time: 4 hours 15 minutes | Prep Time: 30 minutes | Yield: 1 loaf

Ingredients:

1 cup warm water (110°F)	2 tablespoons honey
2 tablespoons olive oil	3 cups bread flour
1 teaspoon salt	1 tablespoon dried basil
1 cup chopped fresh spinach	1/2 cup crumbled feta cheese
2 1/4 teaspoons active dry yeast	

Directions:

(1) Melt the honey and warm water in the bread machine's inner reservoir. Once the honey has dissolved, stir. *(2)* The following ingredients should be added to the pan in the specified order: yeast, chopped spinach, dried basil, olive oil, bread flour, salt, and feta cheese. *(3)* Zojirushi bread machines allow you to choose between "Basic" and "White Bread" settings, where you may also choose the crust color you prefer. *(4)* To initiate the pre-programmed cycles for kneading, rise, and baking in the bread machine, simply depress the start button. *(5)* Once the loaf has been removed from the pan and cooled on a wire tray, section it into segments.

WALNUT AND BLUE CHEESE BREAD

Total Time: 3 hours 30 minutes | Prep Time: 15 minutes

Ingredients:

1 cup warm water (110°F/45°C)	2 tablespoons olive oil
3 cups bread flour	2 tablespoons sugar
1 teaspoon salt	1/2 cup crumbled blue cheese
1/2 cup chopped walnuts	2 1/4 teaspoons active dry yeast

Directions:

(1) Fill the bread pan of your Zojirushi bread machine with olive oil and warm water. *(2)* Toss the bread flour into the water and stir until it dissolves. *(3)* Proceed in the following order: add the salt, sugar, blue cheese, walnuts, and yeast to the bread pan. *(4)* To make white bread, put the bread pan in the bread machine and choose the Basic setting. *(5)* Let the machine do the work of

kneading, rising, and baking the bread. *(6)* When the cycle is finished, carefully take the bread out of the pan and set it on a wire rack to cool before cutting.

CORNBREAD LOAF

Total Time: 2 hours 40 minutes | Prep Time: 10 minutes

Ingredients:

1 cup cornmeal	1 cup all-purpose flour
1 tablespoon baking powder	1/2 teaspoon salt
1/4 cup granulated sugar	1 cup milk
1/4 cup melted butter	2 eggs

Directions:

(1) Fill the bread pan of your Zojirushi bread maker with all the dry ingredients. *(2)* Crack the eggs into the bread pan and stir in the milk and melted butter. Before using the bread machine, put the pan in and choose either the Quick Bread or Cake option. *(3)* Put the cornbread in the machine to bake and mix. Turn it on. *(4)* Carefully take the cornbread out of the pan after the cycle is finished. Allow it to cool before cutting it and serving.

BUTTERMILK BISCUITS

Total Time: 2 hours 20 minutes | Prep Time: 10 minutes

Ingredients:

2 cups all-purpose flour	2 teaspoons baking powder
1/2 teaspoon baking soda	1/2 teaspoon salt
1/4 cup cold unsalted butter, cubed	3/4 cup cold buttermilk
1 tablespoon honey	

Directions:

(1) Fill your Zojirushi bread machine pan with flour, baking powder, baking soda, and salt. *(2)* Butter cubes to flour mixture. *(3)* Add chilled buttermilk and honey to the bread pan. *(4)* Select Dough on the bread maker and place the bread pan. *(5)* Turn on the machine and knead the Dough until smooth and elastic. *(6)* Get out your

parchment paper and preheat your oven to 220°C. Line a baking sheet. *(7)* Roll the Dough 1/2-inch thick on a floured surface. *(8)* Cut biscuits and set them on the baking sheet. *(9)* After 12-15 minutes, the biscuits should be golden brown. *(10)* Warm and serve with butter or jam.

PARMESAN PULL-APART BREAD

Total Time: 3 hours 30 minutes | Prep Time: 15 minutes

Ingredients:

3 cups bread flour	1 tablespoon sugar
1 teaspoon salt	2 tablespoons grated Parmesan cheese
1 1/4 cups warm water (110°F/45°C)	2 1/4 teaspoons active dry yeast
1/4 cup unsalted butter, melted	2 tablespoons chopped fresh parsley

Directions:

(1) Bread flour, sugar, salt, and grated Parmesan cheese go in your Zojirushi bread machine bread pan. *(2)* Add warm water to dry ingredients. *(3)* Add active dry yeast to the bread pan. *(4)* Select Dough on the bread maker and place the bread pan. *(5)* Turn on the machine and knead the Dough until smooth and elastic. *(6)* Grease a 9x5-inch loaf pan and preheat to 350°F (175°C). *(7)* On a lightly floured board, cut the Dough into tiny pieces. *(8)* Put each piece in the loaf pan after rolling it into a ball and dipping it in melted butter. *(9)* Top dough balls with minced parsley. *(10)* Put a clean kitchen towel over the loaf pan and let the Dough rise for 30–45 minutes. *(11)* To get a golden brown crust and a hollow sound when tapped, bake the bread for 30 to 35 minutes. *(12)* The bread needs nine minutes to cool completely after taking it out of the pan on a wire rack.

PRETZEL BUNS

Total Time: 3 hours 20 minutes | Prep Time: 20 minutes

Ingredients:

1 1/2 cups warm water (110°F/45°C)	1 tablespoon granulated sugar
2 1/4 teaspoons active dry yeast	4 cups bread flour
1 teaspoon salt	2 tablespoons baking soda
1 egg, beaten	Coarse salt for topping

Directions:

(1) In your Zojirushi bread machine bread pan, mix warm water, sugar, and active dry yeast. Wait 5-10 minutes for foam. *(2)* Add salt and flour to the bread pan. *(3)* Select Dough and place the bread pan into the bread machine. *(4)* Run the machine to knead the Dough until it is smooth and elastic. *(5)* Roll out a parchment-lined baking sheet and set the oven temperature to 230°C. Form 8 balls from the Dough. *(6)* Boil water and baking soda in a big pot. *(7)* Carefully drop one or two dough balls into hot water and boil for 30 seconds. *(8)* Using a slotted spoon, move the dough balls to the baking sheet. Apply beaten egg and coarse salt to dough balls' tops. *(9)* Bake buns for 12-15 minutes till golden brown. *(10)* Pretzel buns should cool on a wire rack before serving. Enjoy them with your favorite sandwich fillings or hamburger buns.

CHALLAH BREAD

Total Time: 3 hours 30 minutes | Prep Time: 30 minutes | Yield: 1 loaf

Ingredients:

1 cup warm water (110°F)	2 large eggs, room temperature
1/4 cup honey	1/4 cup vegetable oil
4 cups bread flour	1 1/2 teaspoons salt
2 1/4 teaspoons active dry yeast	one egg beaten with one tablespoon of water

Directions:

(1) Fill the bread machine pan with warm water, eggs, honey, and vegetable oil. *(2)* Place bread flour, salt, and active dry yeast on top of the wet ingredients, avoiding water. *(3)* Switch to Dough and start the machine. One round of kneading and rising. *(4)* Transfer the Dough to a floured board and divide it into three equal halves after the dough cycle. *(5)* Roll each piece into a 12-inch

rope. Braide the ropes and tuck the ends to make a loaf. **(6)** After transferring the loaf to a parchment-lined baking sheet, leave it aside to rise in a warm position for one hour or until it has doubled by two. Cover with a clean towel. **(7)** Preheat oven to 375°F (190°C). **(8)** Egg-wash the risen loaf. **(9)** Bake challah for 25–30 minutes until golden brown and hollow when tapped. **(10)** Slice and serve the bread after cooling.

SWEDISH CARDAMOM BREAD

Total Time: 4 hours | Prep Time: 1 hour | Yield: 1 loaf

Ingredients:

1 cup warm milk (110°F)	1/4 cup granulated sugar
1/4 cup unsalted butter, melted	1 large egg, beaten
3 1/2 cups bread flour	1 teaspoon salt
2 teaspoons active dry yeast	2 teaspoons ground cardamom

Directions:

(1) Mix heated milk, sugar, melted butter, and egg in the bread machine pan. **(2)** Adding bread flour, salt, active dry yeast, and ground cardamom to the wet components prevents yeast from touching milk. **(3)** Start the machine with a dough setting. Allow one kneading and rising cycle. **(4)** Place the Dough on a floured board and form it into a loaf after the dough cycle. **(5)** After greasing a loaf pan, place the bread inside and cover it with a clean cloth. **(6)** After about an hour in a warm place, the bread should have doubled in size. Bake at 175 degrees Celsius for at least 15 minutes. The bread should be golden brown and hollow when tapped after 30–35 minutes. **(7)** The bread needs time to cool before it can be served sliced.

IRISH SODA BREAD

Total Time: 1 hour 15 minutes | Prep Time: 15 minutes | Yield: 1 loaf

Ingredients:

3 cups all-purpose flour	1 teaspoon baking soda
1 teaspoon salt	1 1/2 cups buttermilk

Directions:

(1) Set the oven temperature to 425°F, or 220°C. **(2)** To prepare a baking sheet, coat it with cooking spray or utilize parchment paper. Toss the salt, baking soda, and flour together in a large basin. Pour the buttermilk into a well you just made in the middle of the dry ingredients. **(3)** Bring the Dough together by mixing it with a wooden spoon or your hands. You may expect it to be gentle and kind of sticky. **(4)** Using a lightly floured board, shape the Dough into a circular loaf. **(5)** Arrange the bread on the baking sheet that has been preheated. Make a deep cross in the loaf's top with a sharp knife. **(6)** If you want golden brown bread that sounds hollow when tapped, bake it for 30 to 40 minutes. **(7)** After taking the bread out of the oven, let it cool entirely on a wire rack. Now, it's ready to be served.

GERMAN PUMPERNICKEL BREAD

Total Time: 16 hours | Prep Time: 15 minutes | Yield: 1 loaf

Ingredients:

2 cups rye flour	1 cup bread flour
1/4 cup cocoa powder	2 tablespoons molasses
2 tablespoons caraway seeds	1 teaspoon salt
1 1/2 cups warm water	2 1/4 teaspoons active dry yeast

Directions:

(1) The bread machine pan should contain rye flour, bread flour, cocoa powder, molasses, caraway seeds, and salt. **(2)** Mix active dry yeast and warm water in another basin. Let it froth for 5 minutes. **(3)** Transfer yeast mixture to bread machine pan. **(4)** Start the machine on Dough. Knead and raise it once. **(5)** If you oil a loaf pan, you may transfer the Dough when the dough cycle is finished. **(6)** Leave the Dough covered with plastic wrap in a warm place to rise for 8 to 12 hours or until it has doubled in size. **(7)** Turn on the oven to 175°C. **(8)** After 1 hour, the bread should be hard and hollow when tapped. **(9)** Cut and serve the bread after it cools fully.

RUSSIAN BLACK BREAD

Total Time: 3 hours 30 minutes | Prep Time: 30 minutes | Yield: 1 loaf

Ingredients:

1 cup warm water (110°F)	2 tablespoons molasses
2 tablespoons honey	1 tablespoon instant coffee powder
2 tablespoons unsweetened cocoa powder	1 tablespoon caraway seeds
1 teaspoon salt	2 cups bread flour
1 cup rye flour	2 1/4 teaspoons active dry yeast

Directions:

(1) The bread machine pan should contain warm water, molasses, honey, instant coffee powder, cocoa powder, caraway seeds, and salt. **(2)** Place bread flour, rye flour, and active dry yeast on top of the wet ingredients, avoiding water. **(3)** Start the machine with a dough setting. Allow one kneading and rising cycle. **(4)** After the dough cycle, place it in a prepared loaf pan. **(5)** The Dough needs an hour to double in size, so cover the loaf pan with plastic and set it somewhere warm. **(6)** Heat the oven to 190°C. **(7)** Bake until the bread is hard and hollow when tapped, 30–35 minutes. **(8)** The bread needs time to cool before it can be served sliced.

MOROCCAN SEMOLINA BREAD

Total Time: 4 hours 30 minutes | Prep Time: 4 hours | Cook Time: 30 minutes

Ingredients:

1 1/4 cups warm water (110°F/45°C)	2 teaspoons active dry yeast
2 tablespoons honey	3 cups semolina flour
1 teaspoon salt	1/4 cup olive oil
Sesame seeds (optional for topping)	

Directions:

(1) In the bread machine pan, mix warm water, yeast, and honey. Let sit for 5-10 minutes to foam. **(2)** Add semolina flour, salt, and olive oil to the bread machine pan. **(3)** Turn on the dough cycle and press the start button. Give it a little time to rise and knead. **(4)** Take the Dough out of the bread maker and shape it into a loaf or other form. **(5)** Place the formed Dough on a parchment-lined baking sheet. Allow it to rise for another hour under a clean kitchen towel. **(6)** Heat the oven to 190°C. **(7)** Water and sesame seeds can be sprinkled on the rising Dough. **(8)** Preheat oven and bake for 25-30 minutes till golden brown. **(9)** Chill the baked goods on a wire rack prior to dividing and serving.

JAPANESE MILK BREAD

Total Time: 3 hours | Prep Time: 2 hours 30 minutes | Cook Time: 30 minutes

Ingredients:

1 cup warm milk (110°F/45°C)	2 tablespoons unsalted butter, melted
2 tablespoons sugar	3 cups bread flour
2 teaspoons active dry yeast	One teaspoon salt
1 egg, beaten (for egg wash)	

Directions:

(1) Add heated milk, melted butter, and sugar to the bread machine pan. Bread flour, yeast, and salt on top. **(2)** Select the dough cycle and start the machinery. Let it rise and knead for a stipulated time. **(3)** After the dough cycle, remove it from the bread machine and split it into equal shapeable pieces. **(4)** Roll or shape the Dough into a loaf and set it on a greased pan. **(5)** A clean kitchen towel should cover the shaped Dough and let it rise in a warm area for an hour. **(6)** Preheat oven to 350°F (175°C). **(7)** For shine, brush the rising Dough with a beaten egg. **(8)** After 25 to 30 minutes in a preheated oven, check that the bread is golden brown and sounds hollow when tapped. **(9)** Let it cool on a wire rack after baking before serving.

INDIAN NAAN BREAD

Total Time: 2 hours 30 minutes | Prep Time: 2 hours | Cook Time: 30 minutes

Ingredients:

1 cup warm water (110°F/45°C)	2 teaspoons active dry yeast
2 tablespoons sugar	3 cups all-purpose flour

1 teaspoon salt

2 tablespoons ghee or melted butter

Fresh cilantro, chopped (optional, for garnish)

1/4 cup plain yogurt

2 cloves garlic, minced (optional, for garlic naan)

Directions:

(1) In the bread machine pan, mix warm water, yeast, and sugar. Let sit for 5-10 minutes to foam. **(2)** Put the all-purpose flour, salt, yogurt, and ghee or butter in the bread machine pan. **(3)** Turn the machine on and choose the dough cycle. For the time being, let it rise and knead. After the dough cycle, remove it from the bread machine and divide it into equal portions for shaping. **(4)** Each portion of Dough should be oval or circular and 1/4 inch thick. **(5)** When making garlic naan, sprinkle minced garlic evenly over rolled-out Dough and gently press it in. **(6)** Heat a skillet or griddle on medium-high. The rolled-out Dough should be lightly browned and puffed after 2-3 minutes on each side in the skillet. **(7)** Repeat with the remaining Dough. **(8)** Butter and chopped cilantro can be added to baked naan before serving.

MEXICAN CORN TORTILLAS

Total Time: 1 hour 30 minutes | Prep Time: 1 hour 20 minutes | Cook Time: 10 minutes

Ingredients:

2 cups masa harina (corn flour)	1 1/4 cups warm water
1/2 teaspoon salt	

Directions:

(1) In a large basin, mix masa harina and salt. **(2)** Using your hands, gradually add warm water to the masa harina ingredients to make a smooth dough. **(3)** Cut the Dough into pieces about the size of golf balls and keep them covered with a damp towel to keep them from drying out. Prepare a skillet or griddle over medium-high heat. **(4)** Between two parchment or plastic wrap sheets, place a dough ball. Press dough into a thin round tortilla with a tortilla press or heavy plate. **(5)** Remove the tortilla from the parchment paper or plastic wrap and place it on the hot skillet or griddle. **(6)** Cook the tortilla for 1 minute per side until gently browned and done. **(7)** While you make the remaining ingredients, cover the cooked tortilla with a clean kitchen towel to keep it warm. Your favorite fillings or meals go with warm corn tortillas.

CHINESE STEAMED BUNS

Total Time: 2 hours 30 minutes | Prep Time: 2 hours

Ingredients:

1 cup warm water	2 tablespoons sugar
2 teaspoons active dry yeast	3 cups all-purpose flour
1 tablespoon vegetable oil	1 teaspoon salt
½ cup chopped green onions	Filling of your choice (e.g., pork, chicken, vegetables)

Directions:

(1) Warm water, sugar, and yeast should all be combined in the bread machine pan. Wait five minutes for it to get frothy. **(2)** To the pan, add salt, flour, and vegetable oil. **(3)** On your bread machine, select the Dough setting and hit the start button. **(4)** When the Dough is finished, turn it out onto a surface dusted with flour and work in the chopped green onions. **(5)** After dividing the Dough into small balls and flattening each ball into a circle, center each ball with a tablespoon of filling. **(6)** Pinch the Dough's edges shut after folding them over the filling. **(7)** After placing the filled buns on squares of parchment paper, allow them to rise for thirty minutes. **(8)** The buns should be cooked through and puffed after 15 to 20 minutes of steaming in a steamer. **(9)** Enjoy your homemade Chinese steamed buns warm out of the oven!

KOREAN KIMCHI BREAD

Total Time: 3 hours | Prep Time: 2 hours 30 minutes

Ingredients:

1 cup warm milk	2 tablespoons sugar
2 teaspoons active dry yeast	3 cups bread flour
1 tablespoon vegetable oil	1 teaspoon salt

1 cup chopped kimchi	½ cup shredded mozzarella cheese

Directions:

(1) Mix warm milk, sugar, and yeast in the bread machine pan. Wait 5 minutes for foam. **(2)** Place bread flour, vegetable oil, and salt in the pan. **(3)** Select the bread machine dough option and press start. **(4)** Add chopped kimchi and shredded mozzarella cheese to the Dough after the dough cycle. **(5)** Run the dough cycle again and let the bread machine knead the kimchi and cheese. **(6)** Remove the Dough and form it into loaves or rolls after the cycle. **(7)** Let the Dough rise for 30 minutes on a greased baking sheet covered with a cloth. **(8)** Preheat oven to 175°C and bake bread for 25-30 minutes until golden brown. **(9)** Cool the bread before slicing and serving. Eat Korean Kimchi Bread!

THAI COCONUT BREAD

Total Time: 3 hours | Prep Time: 20 minutes

Ingredients:

1 cup coconut milk	2 tablespoons sugar
1 teaspoon salt	3 cups bread flour
2 teaspoons active dry yeast	1/4 cup shredded coconut (optional)

Directions:

(1) In the bread machine pan, mix coconut milk, sugar, and salt. **(2)** Top the liquid mixture with bread flour. **(3)** Make a well in the flour and add yeast. **(4)** Turn on the bread machine's dough cycle. Remove the Dough from the machine and form it into a loaf. **(5)** Once you've buttered a loaf pan, the Dough requires an hour to double in size. While it's rising, cover it with a clean kitchen towel and lay it away in a warm spot. Preheating the oven to 175 degrees Celsius is required. The bread should be golden brown and hollow when tapped after 25–30 minutes. **(6)** Optional: Top the loaf with shredded coconut before baking for texture and taste. **(7)** Slice and serve the bread once it has cooled entirely on a wire rack.

HAWAIIAN POI BREAD

Total Time: 4 hours | Prep Time: 30 minutes

Ingredients:

1 cup poi	1/4 cup honey
2 tablespoons butter, melted	1 teaspoon salt
3 cups bread flour	2 teaspoons active dry yeast

Directions:

(1) Melted butter, poi, honey, and salt should all be combined in the pan of the bread maker. **(2)** Sprinkle the bread flour over the wet mixture. **(3)** In the middle of the flour, create a well and pour in the yeast. **(4)** Start the bread machine by setting it to the dough cycle. **(5)** Take the Dough out of the machine and form it into a loaf after the dough cycle is finished. **(6)** After the Dough has doubled in size, place it in a loaf pan that has been oiled, cover it with a fresh kitchen towel, and let it rise in a warm location for one to two hours. **(7)** Set the oven's temperature to 175°C/350°F. **(8)** The bread should be baked for thirty to thirty-five minutes or until it is golden brown and hollow to the touch. **(9)** To slice and serve, allow the bread to cool completely on a wire rack.

SWEDISH LIMPA BREAD

Total Time: 4 hours 30 minutes | Prep Time: 40 minutes

Ingredients:

1 cup lukewarm water	1/4 cup molasses
2 tablespoons butter, softened	1 teaspoon salt
2 teaspoons caraway seeds	1 teaspoon fennel seeds
1 teaspoon orange zest	3 cups rye flour
1 cup bread flour	2 teaspoons active dry yeast

Directions:

(1) In the bread machine pan, mix lukewarm water, molasses, softened butter, salt, caraway, fennel, and orange zest. **(2)** Sprinkle rye flour over the liquid mixture, then bread flour. **(3)** Put yeast in a flour well. **(4)** Turn on the bread machine's dough cycle. **(5)** After the dough cycle, form it into a loaf outside the machine. **(6)** Grease a loaf pan and line it with a clean kitchen towel to double the Dough's size. Allow to rise for at least an hour and preferably two in a warm spot. **(7)** Turn on the oven to 175°C. **(8)** Bake the bread until golden brown and hollow when tapped, 35-40 minutes. **(9)** Cut and serve the bread after it cools completely on a wire rack.

DANISH RYE BREAD

Total Time: 4 hours 30 minutes | Prep Time: 15 minutes

Ingredients:

1 cup rye flour	2 cups bread flour
1 1/2 teaspoons salt	1 tablespoon caraway seeds
1 tablespoon honey	1 tablespoon molasses
1 cup warm water	2 1/4 teaspoons active dry yeast

Directions:

(1) In your Zojirushi bread machine's bread pan, mix rye flour, bread flour, salt, caraway seeds, honey, molasses, warm water, and yeast. **(2)** Choose "Dough" and hit start. Let the machine knead and raise the Dough for an hour until doubled. **(3)** After the Dough has risen, take it out of the bread machine and form it into a loaf. **(4)** Before letting the Dough rise for half an hour, oil a loaf pan and cover it with a moist kitchen towel. **(5)** Heat the oven to 190°C. **(6)** If you want a golden brown loaf that sounds hollow when tapped, bake it for 30–35 minutes after it has risen. **(7)** Before moving the bread to a wire rack, let it cool for 10 minutes in the pan. Once sliced, serve.

NORWEGIAN POTATO BREAD

Total Time: 3 hours 45 minutes | Prep Time: 20 minutes

Ingredients:

	1 cup mashed potatoes (cooled)
3 cups bread flour	1 tablespoon sugar
1 teaspoon salt	1/4 cup warm water
2 tablespoons unsalted butter	2 1/4 teaspoons active dry yeast

Directions:

(1) Mash potatoes, bread flour, sugar, salt, warm water, butter, and yeast should all be combined in the bread pan of your Zojirushi bread maker. **(2)** Choose "Dough" as the setting, then hit "Start." After the Dough has been kneaded by the machine, give it an hour or so to double in size.

(3) Remove the Dough from the bread maker once it has risen, then roll it into baguettes. Continue to rise the bread for an additional thirty minutes while covering it with a damp kitchen towel, after which transfer it to a loaf pan that has been greased. **(4)** Set the oven temperature to 350°F. **(5)** Bake the risen loaf for thirty to thirty-five minutes or until it is tapped on the bottom and sounds hollow. **(6)** The bread has to sit for ten minutes in the pan before you transfer it to a wire rack to complete cooling. Serve after slicing.

FINNISH PULLA BREAD

Total Time: 4 hours 15 minutes | Prep Time: 25 minutes

Ingredients:

1 cup warm milk	1/2 cup white sugar
1 teaspoon salt	2 eggs
1/2 cup unsalted butter, softened	4 cups bread flour
2 1/4 teaspoons active dry yeast	1/4 cup sliced almonds (optional)
1 egg yolk	1 tablespoon water

Directions:

(1) In your Zojirushi bread machine bread pan, mix warm milk, sugar, salt, eggs, butter, bread flour, and yeast. **(2)** Choose "Dough" and hit start. Let the machine knead and raise the Dough for an hour until doubled. **(3)** After the Dough has risen, take it out of the bread machine and divide it into three equal sections. Make a rope that is fifteen inches long by rolling up each piece. **(4)** Form a loaf by braiding and tucking the ropes. Give the loaf another 30 minutes to rise on a greased baking pan covered with a clean kitchen towel. **(5)** Heat the oven to 175°C. **(6)** Separate the egg yolk from the water in a separate basin. Once the bread has risen, brush it with egg wash and then sprinkle sliced almonds on top. The bread should be golden brown and hollow when tapped after 25–30 minutes. **(7)** After ten minutes, transfer the bread from the oven pan to a wire rack to cool completely. Once sliced, serve.

POLISH BABKA BREAD

Total Time: 4 hours 45 minutes | Prep Time: 30 minutes

Ingredients:

1/2 cup warm milk	1/2 cup white sugar
2 1/4 teaspoons active dry yeast	4 cups bread flour
1 teaspoon salt	1/2 cup unsalted butter, melted
3 eggs	1 teaspoon vanilla extract
1/2 cup raisins	1/4 cup chopped walnuts (optional)
Powdered sugar for dusting	

Directions:

(1) In your Zojirushi bread machine bread pan, mix warm milk, sugar, and yeast. Leave for 5-10 minutes to foam. (2) Bread flour, salt, melted butter, eggs, and vanilla essence in the bread pan. (3) Press start with "Dough" selected. Run the machine and let the Dough rise for an hour until doubled. (4) After the Dough rises, take it from the bread machine and add raisins and chopped walnuts if you are using them. (5) Dividing the Dough in half, form each half into a loaf. After you've greased your loaf pan, set each loaf in it and let it rise for 30 minutes. Cover it with a clean kitchen towel. Preheat oven to 350°F (175°C). (6) The risen loaves should be golden brown and hollow when tapped after 30-35 minutes. (7) Before moving the bread to a wire rack, let it cool for 10 minutes in the pans. Sieve with powdered sugar just before cutting and serving.v

ALBANIAN FLIJA BREAD

Total Time: 3 hours 30 minutes | Prep Time: 30 minutes | Yields: 1 loaf

Ingredients:

2 cups all-purpose flour	1 cup cornmeal
1 teaspoon salt	1 teaspoon sugar
1 packet of active dry yeast	1 cup lukewarm water
Olive oil for greasing	

Directions:

(1) Mix all-purpose flour, cornmeal, salt, and sugar in a large bowl. (2) Dissolve the yeast in the lukewarm water in a small basin and set aside for 5 minutes or until it starts to froth. (3) When a dough forms, whisk in the dry ingredients with

the yeast mixture. (4) To make the Dough smooth and elastic, knead it for 10 minutes on a floured surface. (5) After an hour or two of rising in a warm environment, deflate the Dough by covering it with a kitchen towel and setting it in an oiled basin. (6) Preheat the Zojirushi bread machine to "Bake." (7) Shape a loaf from punched Dough. Use the bread machine pan. (8) Close the lid and choose "Quick Bread." Press "Start". (9) Slice the bread when it has cooled on a wire rack, taking care to remove it from the pan after the cycle is finished.

LEBANESE PITA BREAD

Total Time: 2 hours | Prep Time: 1 hour 30 minutes | Yields: 8 pitas

Ingredients:

3 cups all-purpose flour	1 teaspoon salt
1 tablespoon sugar	1 packet of active dry yeast
1 cup lukewarm water	2 tablespoons olive oil

Directions:

(1) Combine sugar, salt, and all-purpose flour in a gigantic basin. Wait 5 minutes for the yeast to foam in a small basin of lukewarm water. (2) Stir the yeast mixture and olive oil into the dry ingredients to make a dough. (3) Knead floured Dough for 10 minutes until smooth and elastic. (4) Greasing a basin, covering it with a kitchen towel, and letting it rise for an hour in a warm spot can double the Dough's size. Preheat Zojirushi bread maker to "Bake." (5) Shape 8 equal balls of Dough. Form ¼-inch circles from each ball. (6) On the prepared bread machine pan, place dough circles. (7) Select "Bake" and close the lid. Select "Start". (8) Serve the pitas after carefully removing them from the pan and cooling them.

EGYPTIAN AISH BALADI

Total Time: 3 hours 45 minutes | Prep Time: 45 minutes | Yields: 1 loaf

Ingredients:

3 cups whole wheat flour	1 teaspoon salt

1 tablespoon sugar

1 ½ cups lukewarm water

1 packet of active dry yeast

Directions:

(1) Stir together the sugar, salt, and whole wheat flour in a big basin. **(2)** For 5 minutes, or until it becomes frothy, dissolve the yeast in a small basin of lukewarm water. **(3)** Before Dough develops, combine the dry ingredients with the yeast mixture. **(4)** Stretch out the Dough by kneading it for fifteen to twenty minutes on a floured surface. **(5)** After greasing a basin, let the Dough rest for at least two hours, preferably three, or until it has doubled in size. Rest for a while after covering with a dish towel. Start the Zojirushi bread maker on "Bake" mode. **(6)** Punch down and loaf the Dough. The bread machine pans it. **(7)** When the lid is closed, pick the "Quick Bread" cycle. Push "Start". **(8)** Before slicing, let the bread rest on a wire rack after carefully removing it from the pan after baking.

IRANIAN BARBARI BREAD

Total Time: 4 hours | Prep Time: 3 hours 30 minutes | Yields: 2 loaves

Ingredients:

4 cups bread flour	2 teaspoons salt
1 tablespoon sugar	1 packet of active dry yeast
2 cups lukewarm water	Sesame seeds for topping

Directions:

(1) Stir bread flour, salt, and sugar in a large bowl. **(2)** Put yeast in lukewarm water in a small bowl and let it sit for 5 minutes until foamy. **(3)** Add yeast mixture to dry ingredients and mix until dough forms. **(4)** Knead this Dough for 10-15 minutes on a floured surface until smooth and elastic. **(5)** The Dough has to be wrapped in a kitchen towel and placed in an oiled basin. It needs to be left in a warm area for two to three hours to double in size. Turn on the "Bake" setting on your Zojirushi bread machine. Create two equal rectangles out of the Dough, each ½ inch thick. Place dough rectangles on a hot bread machine pan. **(6)** With your fingertips, dimple the Dough and sprinkle sesame seeds. **(7)** Choose

"Bake" and close the lid. Push "Start". **(8)** After the bread has been baked, carefully transfer it to a wire rack to cool. Once cooled, slice it.

AFGHAN NAAN-E-AFGHANI

Total Time: 3 hours 15 minutes | Prep Time: 15 minutes | Yields: 8 pieces

Ingredients:

3 cups all-purpose flour	1 teaspoon salt
1 tablespoon sugar	1 packet of active dry yeast
1 cup lukewarm water	½ cup plain yogurt
2 tablespoons vegetable oil	Nigella seeds, for topping

Directions:

(1) Combine the sugar, salt, and all-purpose flour in a big basin. **(2)** Wait 5 minutes for the yeast to foam in a small basin of lukewarm water. **(3)** Stir the yeast mixture, plain yogurt, and vegetable oil into the dry ingredients to make a dough. **(4)** Knead floured Dough for 10 minutes until smooth and elastic. **(5)** Raise the Dough in a warm spot for one to two hours, or until it has doubled in size, in an oiled basin covered with a kitchen towel. Preheat Zojirushi bread maker to "Bake." **(6)** Shape 8 equal balls of Dough. **(7)** Form ¼-inch circles from each ball. **(8)** On the prepared bread machine pan, place dough circles. **(9)** Toss the Dough with your fingertips and add nigella seeds. **(10)** Select "Bake" and close the lid. Select "Start". **(11)** Before serving, carefully transfer the bread to a wire rack to cool.

PAKISTANI SHEERMAL BREAD

Total Time: 3 hours 30 minutes | Prep Time: 3 hours

Ingredients:

2 cups all-purpose flour	1/4 cup milk
1/4 cup melted ghee (clarified butter)	2 tablespoons sugar
1 teaspoon yeast	1/2 teaspoon salt
1/4 teaspoon saffron strands	1/4 teaspoon cardamom powder
Sliced almonds for garnish	

Directions:

(1) Saffron threads should be dissolved in warm milk. Allow it to cool to lukewarm. (2) Combine flour, sugar, yeast, salt, and cardamom powder in a bowl. (3) Stir the saffron milk and melted ghee into the dry ingredients. Work the Dough until it becomes smooth. (4) The Dough should double in size in about two hours, so cover it with a moist cloth and let it rise. (5) Set your Zojirushi Bread Machine to preheat. (6) Separate the Dough into tiny spheres. Form each ball into the shape of a flatbread. (7) After preheating the machine, place the rolled bread on it and bake it for the recommended amount of time, usually 20 to 25 minutes. (8) When finished, take it out of the machine, brush it with ghee, and top it with almond slices.

NEPALESE SEL ROTI

Total Time: 3 hours | Prep Time: 2 hours | Yields: 8-10 servings

Ingredients:

2 cups rice flour	1 ripe banana, mashed
1 cup sugar	1/2 cup milk
1/4 teaspoon cardamom powder	Oil for deep frying

Directions:

(1) Toss together the rice flour, mashed banana, sugar, milk, and cardamom powder in a big mixing basin. For a smooth batter, mix thoroughly. Wait an hour before adding the batter. (2) Once it has rested, put some oil into a deep fryer and set it over medium heat. (3) With your fingers, form a tiny ring out of a little batter. (4) With caution, drop the batter shapes into the heated oil. Flipping once or twice, fry until golden brown. (5) Once the sel roti is done cooking, remove it from the pan and use paper towels to soak up any extra grease. (6) Use the leftover batter to repeat the procedure. (7) Warm it up and enjoy it with some tea or a sauce of your choice.

BHUTANESE EMA DATSHI BREAD

Total Time: 4 hours | Prep Time: 2.5 hours | Yields: 1 loaf

Ingredients:

3 cups all-purpose flour	1 packet of active dry yeast
1 cup lukewarm water	1 cup grated Bhutanese dashi cheese
2 green chilies, finely chopped	1/2 cup chopped cilantro
1 teaspoon salt	1 tablespoon olive oil

Directions:

(1) Lukewarm water dissolves yeast in a small bowl. Five minutes for froth. (2) Before using, combine the flour and salt in a large bowl. Into the well, carefully add the yeast mixture. (3) Combine flour and water to form Dough. (4) The Dough has to be kneaded in flour for 10 minutes until it becomes elastic. (5) Once the Dough has risen for an hour and a half in an oiled receptacle, transfer it to a clean kitchen towel and allow it to double in volume. (6) Punch the Dough down and add grated dashi cheese, chopped green chilies, and cilantro after rising. (7) Loaf in a greased pan. Leave covered for 30 minutes to rise. (8) Start the Zojirushi breadmaker on "Bake." (9) Place dough in a bread machine with olive oil. (10) After 30–40 minutes, the bread should sound hollow and golden brown. (11) The bread is sliced after cooling on a wire rack. (12) Put Bhutanese Ema Datshi Bread with your favorite broth or stew.

TIBETAN TINGMO BREAD

Total Time: 3 hours 30 minutes | Prep Time: 30 minutes

Ingredients:

3 cups all-purpose flour	1 tablespoon active dry yeast
1 tablespoon sugar	1 teaspoon salt
1 cup warm water	

Directions:

(1) Whisk together the yeast, sugar, and warm water in a mixing dish. Wait five to ten minutes for it to get foamy. (2) Sift the flour and salt in a different bowl. (3) After kneading the Dough until it becomes elastic and smooth, incorporate the flour mixture into the yeast mixture gradually. (4) Once the Dough has doubled in size, place it in a warm position and allow it to rise for around two hours. Place a damp cloth over the top. After pounding the Dough, separate

it into tiny balls. *(5)* Form each ball into a circle that is approximately 1/4 inch thick. *(6)* After lining a tray with parchment paper, place the circles in the Zojirushi bread maker and steam for 15 to 20 minutes or until they are cooked through. *(7)* Warm up and enjoy with your favorite foods.

MONGOLIAN BOORTSOG BREAD

Total Time: 2 hours | Prep Time: 1 hour

Ingredients:

3 cups all-purpose flour	1 teaspoon baking powder
1/2 teaspoon salt	1/4 cup unsalted butter, melted
1/2 cup warm water	Oil for frying

Directions:

(1) When combining flour, baking powder, and salt, a big mixing basin is a way to go. *(2)* After the Dough has come together smoothly, knead in the melted butter and warm water a little at a time. *(3)* The Dough needs thirty minutes to rest, so cover it with a damp cloth. *(4)* The Dough can be rolled out into a thin sheet and then cut into the required shapes, such as little rectangles. *(5)* Toss in oil and heat to 350°F (180°C) in a deep fryer or skillet. *(6)* Fry in batches, giving each batch of Dough pieces two to three minutes on each side or until golden brown and crispy. *(7)* Take it out and place it on paper towels to drain from the oil. *(8)* Warm or room temperature, serve Boortsog bread with jam or honey.

KAZAKH BAURSAKI BREAD

Total Time: 2 hours 30 minutes | Prep Time: 1 hour

Ingredients:

2 cups all-purpose flour	1 teaspoon baking powder
1/2 teaspoon salt	2 tablespoons unsalted butter, melted
1/2 cup milk	Oil for frying

Directions:

(1) It is optimal to combine flour, baking powder, and salt in a large mixing basin. After the Dough has come together well, mix in the melted butter and milk a little at a time. After an hour of resting, cover the Dough with a damp cloth. *(2)* Toss in oil and heat to 350°F (180°C) in a deep fryer or skillet. *(3)* Form the Dough into little balls or squares by pinching off tiny bits of the Dough. *(4)* Slices of Dough should be fried in batches for two to three minutes on each side or until they are cooked through and golden brown. *(5)* Take it out and place it on paper towels to drain from the oil. *(6)* With tea or coffee, serve warm Baursaki bread.

GEORGIAN SHOTI BREAD

Total Time: 4 hours | Prep Time: 3 hours

Ingredients:

4 cups all-purpose flour	1 tablespoon active dry yeast
1 teaspoon sugar	1 teaspoon salt
1 1/2 cups warm water	

Directions:

(1) Warm water, yeast, and sugar are combined in a large basin. It should start to foam within five to ten minutes. *(2)* Sift the flour and salt in an individual dish. *(3)* Post-combine the yeast and flour mixtures and knead the Dough until it reaches a uniform and elastic consistency. *(4)* The Dough should rise in a warm location for about two hours or until it has doubled in size. Cover the Dough with a moist cloth. *(5)* The Dough is pounded down and then shaped into tiny balls. *(6)* Each ball should be rolled out into an oval form that is 1/4 inch thick. *(7)* Set the Zojirushi bread maker to "bake" mode before using it. *(8)* After the machine is hot, place the rolled Dough on it and bake for 15 to 20 minutes or until it is cooked through and golden brown. *(9)* Warm-shot bread goes well with your preferred Georgian cuisine.

ARMENIAN LAVASH BREAD

Total Time: 2 hours 30 minutes | Prep Time: 1 hour

Ingredients:

3 cups all-purpose flour	1 teaspoon salt
1 tablespoon olive oil	1 cup warm water

Directions:

(1) In a basin, combine the flour and salt. (2) Following this, knead the tepid water and olive oil into the dry ingredients in a gradual motion until a cohesive dough is produced. (3) For one hour, cover the Dough with a moist cloth and let it rest. (4) Adjust the Zojirushi bread maker's temperature to "bake" before use. (5) Roll out the Dough into thin sheets after dividing it into small sections. (6) The rolled Dough should be baked for ten to fifteen minutes or until crispy and golden brown in the preheated machine. (7) Take it out of the machine and let it cool down a little before serving. (8) Serve Lavash bread as a sandwich wrapper or with spreads and dips.

AZERBAIJANI TANDIR BREAD

Total Time: 4 hours 30 minutes | Prep Time: 4 hours

Ingredients:

4 cups all-purpose flour	1 teaspoon salt
1 tablespoon sugar	2 teaspoons active dry yeast
1 ½ cups warm water	

Directions:

(1) Grease the flour, sugar, and salt together in a large basin. After dissolving the yeast in warm water, give it five minutes to reach a frothy consistency. (2) Be sure to knead the Dough until it's smooth after adding the yeast mixture to the flour mixture. (3) Cover the Dough with a clean kitchen towel and set it aside in a warm place to rest for two hours once it has doubled in size. (4) Set the Zojirushi bread maker to preheat. (5) Shape each of the two equal portions of Dough into a round loaf. (6) After adding the Dough, choose the "Bake" setting on the bread machine. (7) Bake for 30 to 35 minutes, or until the bread is hollow when tapped on the bottom and has a golden brown color. (8) Once the bread has cooled on a wire rack, remove it from the machine and slice it.

BELARUSIAN DRANIKI BREAD

Total Time: 3 hours 15 minutes | Prep Time: 3 hours

Ingredients:

3 cups grated potatoes	1 onion, finely chopped
2 eggs, beaten	½ cup all-purpose flour
Salt and pepper to taste	

Directions:

(1) Grated potatoes, chopped onion, eggs that have been beaten, flour, salt, and pepper should be mixed together in a sizeable basin. (2) Perform a thorough mixing until all of the components are uniformly distributed. (3) Bring the Zojirushi bread machine up to temperature. (4) After lubricating the bread pan, evenly distribute the potato mixture across the pan's bottom. (5) Make sure that the bread machine is set to the "Bake" setting, and then bake it for thirty to thirty-five minutes or until the exterior of the bread is golden brown and crispy. (6) After taking the bread out of the machine, allow it to cool down for a short while before slicing it.

ESTONIAN LEIB BREAD

Total Time: 4 hours 45 minutes | Prep Time: 4 hours 30 minutes

Ingredients:

3 cups rye flour	1 cup all-purpose flour
1 tablespoon caraway seeds	2 teaspoons salt
1 tablespoon molasses	2 cups warm water
2 teaspoons active dry yeast	

Directions:

(1) Caraway seeds, salt, rye flour, and all-purpose flour should all be combined in a big mixing basin. (2) After dissolving molasses in warm water, top with yeast. Until foamy, let it sit for five minutes. (3) Be sure to knead the Dough until it's smooth after adding the yeast mixture to the flour mixture. The Dough should double in size after four hours of rising in a warm location when covered with a fresh kitchen towel. (4) Set the Zojirushi bread maker to preheat. (5) Before placing the Dough into the bread machine, shape it into a circular loaf. When the bread is solid and sounds hollow when tapped on the bottom, bake

it for 45 to 50 minutes on the "Bake" setting. *(6)* Once the bread has cooled on a wire rack, remove it from the machine and slice it.

LATVIAN RUPJMAIZE BREAD

Total Time: 4 hours | Prep Time: 20 minutes

Ingredients:

1 1/2 cups rye flour	1 1/2 cups bread flour
1 cup lukewarm water	1/4 cup molasses
2 tablespoons caraway seeds	1 tablespoon active dry yeast
1 teaspoon salt	

Directions:

(1) Melted butter, molasses, and yeast should all be combined in the pan of the bread maker. After the yeast has had five minutes to activate and foam, let it sit. *(2)* Toss in the caraway seeds, rye flour, bread flour, and salt. *(3)* If the desired crust color is available, select it along with the "Basic" or "Whole Wheat" cycle on your Zojirushi bread maker. *(4)* Set the machine to the desired cycle and let it knead, rise, and bake the bread. *(5)* Drain the bread from the pan using a wire rack prior to slicing once the cycle has concluded. *(6)* Savor the robust taste of Latvian Rupjmaize Bread with your preferred spreads or substantial soups and stews.

RUSSIAN KULICH BREAD

Total Time: 6 hours | Prep Time: 30 minutes

Ingredients:

3 cups bread flour	1/2 cup warm milk
1/4 cup granulated sugar	1/4 cup unsalted butter, melted
2 eggs	1/4 cup golden raisins
1/4 cup chopped almonds	1/4 cup chopped candied citrus peel
2 tablespoons rum (optional)	1 tablespoon active dry yeast
1 teaspoon vanilla extract	1/2 teaspoon salt
Confectioners' sugar for dusting	

Directions:

(1) If using, soak golden raisins, chopped almonds, and chopped candied citrus peel in rum for 15 minutes in a small basin. *(2)* Mix warm milk, melted butter, sugar, eggs, yeast, vanilla extract, and salt in the bread machine pan. *(3)* Put bread flour in the pan. *(4)* Drain and add soaking fruits and nuts to the pan. *(5)* Use the "Sweet" or "Cake" cycle on your Zojirushi bread machine and select the crust color if available. *(6)* Start the machine and let it knead, rise, and bake the bread per the cycle. *(7)* Carefully remove the bread from the pan once the cycle is finished, and let it cool on a wire rack. Sprinkle confectioners' sugar on cooled Kulich Bread before serving. This classic Russian bread is a delicious Easter treat or a year-round sweet treat.

HUNGARIAN KALÁCS BREAD

Total Time: 3 hours 30 minutes | Prep Time: 30 minutes | Yield: 1 loaf

Ingredients:

1 cup warm milk	2 ¼ teaspoons active dry yeast
¼ cup granulated sugar	3 ½ cups all-purpose flour
1 teaspoon salt	2 eggs
½ cup unsalted butter melted	½ cup apricot jam
½ cup chopped walnuts	1 tablespoon grated lemon zest

Directions:

(1) In a little bowl, combine the yeast, warm milk, and a quarter teaspoon of sugar. Allow 5 to 10 minutes for foam to form. *(2)* Grease the flour, salt, and sugar together in a large bowl. After excavating a well, softened butter, eggs, and yeast are added to it. *(3)* Stir in the flour after bringing the remaining ingredients to a boil; continue mixing until the Dough forms a ball. Approximately five to seven minutes, or until the Dough becomes elastic and smooth, knead the Dough. *(4)* Let the Dough rise in a greased basin with a clean cloth for 1–1.5 hours until doubled. *(5)* Punch Dough and divide it into three equal halves. Rolled rectangles. *(6)* Chopped walnuts and lemon zest go on each rectangle after the apricot jam. *(7)* Form a tight log from each rectangle, braid, and tuck. *(8)* Cover the braided

loaf while it rises for thirty minutes on a baking sheet lined with parchment paper. The "Bake" operational option is characteristic of the Zojirushi bread machine. *(9)* Place the loaf carefully in the bread machine and bake for 25–30 minutes until golden brown and hollow when tapped. *(10)* Slice and serve cooled bread.

CZECH VÁNOČKA BREAD

Total Time: 4 hours | Prep Time: 1 hour 30 minutes | Yield: 1 loaf

Ingredients:

1 cup warm milk	2 ¼ teaspoons active dry yeast
½ cup granulated sugar	4 cups all-purpose flour
1 teaspoon salt	3 eggs
½ cup unsalted butter melted	½ cup golden raisins
½ cup chopped almonds	1 tablespoon grated orange zest
1 egg yolk, beaten (for egg wash)	

Directions:

(1) In a little bowl, combine the yeast, warm milk, and a quarter teaspoon of sugar. Keep aside 5 to 10 minutes for foaming. *(2)* A considerable amount of flour, salt, and sugar are combined in a receptacle. Yeast, eggs, and butter-flour are combined in a well. Once the ingredients have been combined with a stir, knead the Dough on a floured surface for 10 minutes or until it reaches a smooth and elastic consistency. *(3)* Proceed to allow the Dough to double in volume, approximately 1.5-2 hours, by placing it in a greased receptacle covered with a cloth and placing it in a warm location. Punch down Dough and evenly distribute golden raisins, chopped almonds, and grated orange zest. *(4)* A parchment-lined baking pan should hold a round loaf of Dough. Let rise covered for 30–45 minutes. *(5)* Prepare the Zojirushi Bread Machine for "Bake." *(6)* Brush beaten egg yolk on the loaf after preheating for shine. *(7)* Carefully put the loaf in the bread machine and bake for 35–40 minutes until golden brown and hollow upon tapping. *(8)* Slice and serve the bread after cooling.

SLOVAK PASKA BREAD

Total Time: 4 hours 30 minutes | Prep Time: 2 hours | Yield: 1 loaf

Ingredients:

1 cup warm milk	2 ¼ teaspoons active dry yeast
½ cup granulated sugar	4 cups all-purpose flour
1 teaspoon salt	3 eggs
½ cup unsalted butter melted	½ cup golden raisins
½ cup chopped pecans	1 tablespoon grated lemon zest
1 teaspoon vanilla extract	

Directions:

(1) Stir warm milk, yeast, and a pinch of sugar in a small bowl. Wait 5-10 minutes for froth. *(2)* Salt, flour, and sugar are incorporated into a sizable bowl. In a well, combine the yeast mixture, melted butter, eggs, and vanilla extract. *(3)* After the Dough has formed, knead it for 10 to 12 minutes on a floured surface until it is smooth and elastic. *(4)* To facilitate doubling, place the Dough in an oiled receptacle and cover it with a clean cloth for two hours in a warm location. *(5)* Punch down the Dough and evenly distribute golden raisins, chopped pecans, and grated lemon zest. *(6)* Using parchment paper, shape the Dough into a circular loaf and set it on a baking sheet. Set aside for 30–45 minutes with the cover on. Start the Zojirushi Bread Machine on "Bake" mode. *(7)* Carefully transfer the loaf to the bread machine and bake for 40–45 minutes until golden brown and hollow when tapped. *(8)* Slice and serve the bread after cooling.

CROATIAN POVITICA BREAD

Total Time: 5 hours | Prep Time: 2 hours 30 minutes | Yield: 1 loaf

Ingredients:

1 cup warm milk	2 ¼ teaspoons active dry yeast
¼ cup granulated sugar	3 ½ cups all-purpose flour
1 teaspoon salt	2 eggs
½ cup unsalted butter melted	1 cup walnut halves

½ cup granulated sugar	1 teaspoon ground cinnamon
1 tablespoon rum or brandy	

Directions:

(1) A small bowl with warm milk, yeast, and a pinch of sugar. Wait 5-10 minutes for foam. **(2)** Put flour, sugar, and salt in a big bowl. Add eggs, melted butter, and yeast to a well. **(3)** When the Dough is mixed, knead it for five to seven minutes on a floured surface or until it becomes elastic and smooth. **(4)** After greasing a basin, set aside the Dough to rise for 1.5 to 2 hours, covered with a clean towel, until it has multiplied by two. **(5)** Combine walnut halves, sugar, cinnamon, and rum/brandy. Pulverize fine. **(6)** On floured ground, make a large rectangle. **(7)** Apply the walnut mixture to the Dough. **(8)** Tightly roll out the Dough, starting from the longest side. Keep the rolled Dough covered with parchment paper for 30–45 minutes to rise. **(9)** Set the Zojirushi Bread Machine to "Bake." **(10)** Place the loaf carefully in the preheated bread machine and bake for 50–55 minutes until golden brown and hollow when tapped. **(11)** After cooling, slice and serve the bread.

BOSNIAN SOMUN BREAD

Total Time: 3 hours | Prep Time: 1 hour 30 minutes | Yield: 4 loaves

Ingredients:

2 cups warm water	2 ¼ teaspoons active dry yeast
1 tablespoon sugar	5 cups bread flour
1 teaspoon salt	

Directions:

(1) Take a small bowl and combine the yeast, sugar, and warm water. To achieve foaming, wait 5 to 10 minutes. **(2)** A large bowl is ideal for mixing the flour and salt. Combine the yeast mixture and fill a well. Mix to create a dough, then knead for 10-12 minutes on a floured surface until smooth and elastic. **(3)** Form four balls from the Dough. **(4)** Allow the Dough balls to rise on a baking sheet lined with paper for at least an hour, covered, until they have doubled in size. **(5)** Preheat the Zojirushi Bread Machine to

"Bake." **(6)** Preheat the bread machine and carefully transfer the dough balls. Bake for 20–25 minutes until golden brown and hollow when tapped. **(7)** Before cutting and serving, let the bread cool.

SLOVENIAN POTICA BREAD

Total Time: 4 hours 30 minutes | Prep Time: 30 minutes

Ingredients:

1 cup warm milk	1/2 cup sugar
1/4 cup melted butter	2 large eggs
4 cups all-purpose flour	2 1/4 teaspoons active dry yeast
1/2 teaspoon salt	1 cup finely chopped walnuts
1/2 cup raisins	1/4 cup honey
1 teaspoon ground cinnamon	

Directions:

(1) Melted butter, sugar, eggs, and warm milk should all be combined in the bread machine pan. **(2)** To the pan, add the flour, yeast, and salt. **(3)** Choose the dough cycle and hit the start button. **(4)** After the dough cycle is finished, place the Dough on a surface dusted with flour and allow it to rest for ten minutes. **(5)** Combine the walnuts, raisins, honey, and cinnamon in a small bowl. **(6)** The Dough should be rolled out into a big rectangle. **(7)** Evenly distribute the walnut mixture onto the Dough. **(8)** Tightly roll the Dough and put it seam-side down in a loaf pan that has been oiled. **(9)** Place a fresh towel over it and let it rise for an hour in a warm location. **(10)** Set the oven's temperature to 175°C/350°F. **(11)** Bake for thirty to thirty-five minutes or until golden brown. **(12)** Let the bread cool down before cutting into slices and serving.

MONTENEGRIN POGAČA BREAD

Total Time: 3 hours 45 minutes | Prep Time: 15 minutes

Ingredients:

1 1/4 cups warm water	2 tablespoons olive oil
1 tablespoon sugar	1 teaspoon salt

3 cups bread flour	2 1/4 teaspoons active dry yeast
2 tablespoons chopped fresh rosemary	Coarse sea salt for topping

Directions:

(1) In the pan of the bread machine, combine the olive oil, sugar, salt, and warm water. **(2)** Toss in the yeast and bread flour in the pan. **(3)** Choose the dough cycle and hit the start button. **(4)** After the dough cycle concludes, place the Dough in a greased container, cover it, and set it aside to rise for one hour in a warm environment. **(5)** Separate the Dough into eight equal pieces after punching it down. **(6)** Subsequently, shape each portion into a ball on a parchment-lined baking sheet. **(7)** After slightly flattening the spheres, sprinkle minced rosemary and coarse sea salt on top. **(8)** After an additional thirty minutes, proceed with the emergence of the items by covering them with a clean towel. **(9)** At 200°C, preheat the oven to high heat. Turn the bread over and bake it for another 15 to 20 minutes or until it turns a golden finish. **(10)** Graze when hot and savor!

MACEDONIAN POGACHA BREAD

Total Time: 3 hours 30 minutes | Prep Time: 30 minutes | Cook Time: 3 hours

Ingredients:

1 cup warm water	2 teaspoons active dry yeast
1 tablespoon sugar	3 cups all-purpose flour
1 teaspoon salt	2 tablespoons olive oil
1 tablespoon yogurt	Sesame seeds for topping (optional)

Directions:

(1) Yeast, sugar, and tepid water are combined in a small basin. Allow five to ten minutes to froth. **(2)** Together, flour and salt in a large basin. Centralize effectively. **(3)** In a well, combine olive oil, yogurt, and yeast. **(4)** After combining the ingredients, the Dough should be kneaded for 5 to 7 minutes on a floured surface or until elastic and smooth. **(5)** The Dough should double in 1-2 hours in a greased basin covered with a clean dish towel. **(6)** Start the Zojirushi bread machine

in "Dough" mode. **(7)** After rising, punch down and split the Dough in half. Making circular loaves from each half. **(8)** Let loaves rise on parchment-lined baking sheets for 30–45 minutes. **(9)** Set the oven to 190°C. **(10)** Adding water and sesame seeds to the bread is optional. **(11)** After 25-30 minutes, the bottom should be hollow and golden brown. **(12)** Cool the bread on a wire rack, then slice and serve.

BULGARIAN BANITSA BREAD

Total Time: 4 hours | Prep Time: 1 hour | Cook Time: 3 hours

Ingredients:

1 package active dry yeast	1/4 cup warm water
1 tablespoon sugar	4 cups all-purpose flour
1 teaspoon salt	1/2 cup melted butter, divided
1 cup lukewarm milk	2 eggs
1 cup crumbled feta cheese	1/4 cup chopped fresh parsley
Additional melted butter for brushing	

Directions:

(1) Warm water with yeast and sugar combined in a small basin. To froth, soak for 5 to 10 minutes. **(2)** Salt and flour in a big basin. Dig a central well. **(3)** Combine yeast, 1/4 cup melted butter, lukewarm milk, and eggs in the well. **(4)** For 5 to 7 minutes, knead the Dough on a floured surface until it is elastic and smooth. **(5)** Wait 1-2 hours for the Dough to double in an oiled bowl with a clean kitchen towel. **(6)** Put the Zojirushi bread maker in "Dough" mode. **(7)** Post-rising, punch down and split the Dough in half. **(8)** Make 1/4-inch rectangles from each portion. **(9)** Melt butter and sprinkle feta and parsley on Dough. **(10)** Roll and spiralize each rectangle. **(11)** Spirals should rise on a parchment-lined baking sheet for 30–45 minutes. **(12)** Heat oven to 350°F (175°C). **(13)** Take 30–35 minutes to brown. **(14)** Recoat with melted butter when heated. **(15)** Cold bread is needed for slicing and serving.

ROMANIAN COZONAC BREAD

Total Time: 5 hours | Prep Time: 1 hour | Cook Time: 4 hours

Ingredients:

1 package active dry yeast	1/4 cup warm water
1 tablespoon sugar	4 cups all-purpose flour
1/2 cup sugar	1 teaspoon salt
1/2 cup melted butter	3 eggs
1/2 cup milk	1 teaspoon vanilla extract
1 cup chopped walnuts	1 cup raisins
Zest of 1 lemon	Zest of 1 orange
Additional melted butter for brushing	

Directions:

(1) Place yeast and 1 tablespoon sugar in a small bowl of warm water. Allow 5-10 minutes of foaming. (2) Salt, flour, and 1/2 cup sugar in a large bowl. Clear the well. (3) The well should contain yeast, melted butter, eggs, milk, and vanilla. (4) After mixing, knead the Dough for 5-7 minutes on a floured surface until elastic. (5) Grease a receptacle, cover it with a clean kitchen towel, and position it in a warm location for one to two hours in order to double the Dough. (6) Use "Dough" mode on your Zojirushi bread machine. (7) When the Dough rises, pound it and distribute chopped walnuts, raisins, lemon zest, and orange zest. (8) Make loaves from each half of the Dough. (9) Set the loaves in oiled loaf pans to rise for 1–2 hours. (10) Turn on the oven to 175°C. (11) Finish baking 30–40 minutes until browned. (12) Warmly butter the loaves' tops. (13) After ten minutes, transfer the bread to a wire rack to finish chilling.

ALBANIAN PITE BREAD

Total Time: 4 hours | Prep Time: 30 minutes | Yield: 1 loaf

Ingredients:

1 1/4 cups warm water	2 teaspoons active dry yeast
1 tablespoon sugar	3 cups all-purpose flour
1 teaspoon salt	1/4 cup olive oil

1 egg, beaten (for egg wash)	Black sesame seeds for topping (optional)

Directions:

(1) Warm water, yeast, and sugar are combined in the pan of the Zojirushi bread machine. Ten to fifteen minutes to froth. (2) Salt, flour, and olive oil are combined in a saucepan. (3) To begin, operate your bread machine and select the Dough preset. (4) Take the Dough out of the machine and set it on a lightly floured surface. (5) Preheat oven to 375°F (190°C). (6) Two equal quantities of Dough should be shaped into circular loaves. (7) The bread should be transferred to a baking tray lined with parchment. (8) When desired, garnish the bread with black sesame seeds and a whisked egg. (9) Over a moderate environment, allow the bread to rise for 30 minutes. (10) Twenty-five to thirty minutes, or until golden brown and hollow when tapped. (11) Slice and serve the bread when it cools on a wire rack.

WHOLE WHEAT SANDWICH LOAF

Total Time: 3 hours 45 minutes | Prep Time: 15 minutes | Yield: 1 loaf

Ingredients:

1 1/4 cups warm water	2 teaspoons active dry yeast
2 tablespoons honey	3 cups whole wheat flour
1 teaspoon salt	1/4 cup olive oil
1 tablespoon rolled oats (for topping)	

Directions:

(1) Mix warm water, yeast, and honey in the Zojirushi bread machine pan. Wait 5-10 minutes for frothing. (2) Put whole wheat flour, salt, and olive oil in the pan. (3) Set your bread machine to whole wheat and start. (4) After the bread machine cycle, form the Dough into a loaf. (5) It takes thirty minutes at a mild temperature, with the Dough rising in an oiled loaf pan covered with a clean kitchen towel. (6) Heat the oven to 175°C. (7) Top the bread with rolled oats. (8) After 30–35 minutes, the bottom should sound hollow and golden brown. (9) Allow the bread to

settle in the pan for ten minutes prior to transferring it to a wire tray.

HONEY OAT BREAD

Total Time: 3 hours 30 minutes | Prep Time: 15 minutes | Yield: 1 loaf

Ingredients:

1 cup warm water	2 tablespoons honey
1 tablespoon olive oil	1 teaspoon salt
2 1/2 cups bread flour	1/2 cup rolled oats
2 teaspoons active dry yeast	

Directions:

(1) Get the honey, olive oil, salt, and warm water into the bread machine's pan. *(2)* Position the active dry yeast above the bread flour and rolled oats, making sure it does not come into contact with the liquids. *(3)* To make a 2-pound loaf with a thin crust, put the pan into the bread maker and put it on the Basic or White Bread setting. *(4)* Let the bread machine begin its cycle. *(5)* After the baking cycle ends, carefully take the bread out of the pan and set it on a wire rack to cool while you cut it.

SOURDOUGH BREAD

Total Time: 12 to 18 hours (including resting time) | Prep Time: 15 minutes | Yield: 1 loaf

Ingredients:

1 cup active sourdough starter	1 1/2 cups bread flour
1/2 cup whole wheat flour	1 teaspoon salt
1 tablespoon olive oil	Cornmeal (for dusting)

Directions:

(1) In a large basin, mix active sourdough starter, bread flour, whole wheat flour, salt, and olive oil. Form dough by mixing. *(2)* 5-7 minutes on a lightly floured surface will make the Dough smooth and elastic. *(3)* The Dough will double in size when left at room temperature for eight to twelve hours in a lightly lubricated receptacle covered with a clean kitchen towel. Following a doubling process, the Dough should be gently compressed and shaped into a baguette. *(4)* Carefully place the formed Dough in the bread machine pan after cornmealing it. *(5)* Set the bread maker to Sourdough and place the pan in. *(6)* Launch the breadmaker. *(7)* Before dividing, allow the bread to chill on a wire rack following baking.

PUMPERNICKEL BREAD

Total Time: 3 hours 30 minutes | Prep Time: 15 minutes

Ingredients:

1 cup water	2 tablespoons vegetable oil
2 tablespoons molasses	1 1/2 teaspoons salt
1 cup rye flour	2 cups bread flour
1 tablespoon cocoa powder	1 tablespoon caraway seeds
2 teaspoons active dry yeast	

Directions:

(1) Put all of the ingredients into the pan of the bread machine in the order that the manufacturer suggests the ingredients be placed. *(2)* The "Basic" or "Whole Wheat" cycle, together with the crust setting that you prefer, should be selected. *(3)* Give the bread machine a start, and then sit back and watch it do its thing. *(4)* The bread should be removed from the pan once the cycle is finished, and it should be let to cool on a wire rack before being sliced. *(5)* Have delicious and freshly baked pumpernickel bread from us!

GARLIC HERB BREAD

Total Time: 3 hours 45 minutes | Prep Time: 20 minutes

Ingredients:

1 1/4 cups warm water	2 tablespoons olive oil
3 cloves garlic, minced	3 cups bread flour
1 tablespoon sugar	1 1/2 teaspoons salt
2 teaspoons dried basil	1 teaspoon dried oregano
2 teaspoons active dry yeast	

Directions:

(1) Olive oil, heated water, and minced garlic should be combined in the bread machine's receptacle. Incorporate the following Ingredients: bread flour, sugar, salt, dried oregano, dried basil, and active dry yeast. (2) Make sure to choose the "Basic" or "White Bread" cycle, as well as the crust setting that you prefer. (3) Upon activating the start button, the bread machine will initiate the process of Dough combining, kneading, rising, and baking. A wire rack should be used to allow the bread to cool after it has been removed from the pan after the cycle has been completed. (4) Garlic Herb Bread is a fragrant bread that may be sliced and served with your other favorite foods.

CHEESE AND HERB BREAD

Total Time: 3 hours 30 minutes | Prep Time: 15 minutes

Ingredients:

1 cup warm milk	1/4 cup melted butter
2 cups bread flour	1 cup shredded cheddar cheese
1 tablespoon dried parsley	1 teaspoon garlic powder
1 teaspoon onion powder	2 teaspoons active dry yeast
1 teaspoon sugar	1 teaspoon salt

Directions:

(1) The bread machine pan should be filled with warm milk and melted butter. (2) Incorporate the following ingredients into the mixture: bread flour, shredded cheddar cheese, dried parsley, garlic powder, onion powder, active dry yeast, sugar, and salt. (3) Make sure to choose the "Basic" or "White Bread" cycle, as well as the crust setting that you prefer. (4) The Dough should be baked until it is fragrant and golden brown, after which the bread machine should be started and allowed to mix, knead, and rise. (5) After it is finished cooking, proceed to remove the bread from the pan with caution and place it on a wire rack to cool. (6) This wonderful Cheese and Herb Bread can be served warm with butter or alongside your favorite soups and salads, depending on your preference.

JALAPENO CHEDDAR BREAD

Total Time: 3 hours 45 minutes | Prep Time: 20 minutes

Ingredients:

1 cup warm water	2 tablespoons olive oil
3 tablespoons chopped pickled jalapenos	2 cups bread flour
1 cup shredded cheddar cheese	2 teaspoons sugar
1 1/2 teaspoons salt	Two teaspoons of active dry yeast

Directions:

(1) The pan of the bread machine should be filled with warm water, olive oil, and pickled jalapenos that have been diced. (2) Be sure to include active dry yeast, sugar, salt, shredded cheddar cheese, and bread flour in the mixture. (3) Make sure to choose the "Basic" or "White Bread" cycle, as well as the crust setting that you prefer. (4) Get the bread machine started, and then allow it to handle the mixing, kneading, rising, and baking of the Dough. (5) A wire rack should be used to allow the Jalapeno Cheddar Bread to cool when it has been removed from the machine after the cycle has been completed. (6) This spicy and cheesy bread can be enjoyed on its own or as a savory addition to any meal. This bread can be sliced and served.

SUN-DRIED TOMATO BREAD

Total Time: 3 hours 45 minutes | Prep Time: 20 minutes

Ingredients:

1 1/4 cups warm water	2 tablespoons olive oil
1/2 cup chopped sun-dried tomatoes	3 cups bread flour
1 teaspoon sugar	1 1/2 teaspoons salt
2 teaspoons dried basil	2 teaspoons active dry yeast

Directions:

(1) Toss chopped sun-dried tomatoes with olive oil, warm water, and the bread machine. (2) To the flour, add the sugar, salt, dried basil, and active dry yeast. Mix well. (3) Choose between the "Basic" and "White Bread" cycles, then adjust

the crust setting to your liking. *(4)* Get the bread machine going and let it do all the work: mixing, kneading, rising, and baking the Dough until it's nice and toasty and smells good. *(5)* After the Sun-Dried Tomato Bread is finished, take it out of the machine and set it on a wire rack to cool. *(6)* Slices of this fragrant bread can be used to top salads and soups or make a delectable sandwich.

OLIVE AND ROSEMARY BREAD

Total Time: 3 hours 30 minutes | Prep Time: 15 minutes | Yield: 1 loaf

Ingredients:

1 cup warm water	2 tablespoons olive oil
3 cups bread flour	2 teaspoons sugar
1 1/2 teaspoons salt	1 tablespoon dried rosemary
1/2 cup chopped pitted kalamata olives	2 1/4 teaspoons active dry yeast

Directions:

(1) Following the manufacturer-recommended sequence, add the following ingredients to the bread machine pan: warm water, olive oil, bread flour, sugar, salt, dried rosemary, chopped olives, and active dry yeast. *(2)* To make a 1.5-pound loaf with a color crust of your choice, put your bread machine in Basic or White Bread mode. *(3)* Roll out the bread. *(4)* After the baking time is up, gently take the loaf out of the oven and set it on a wire rack to cool before cutting. *(5)* Olive and rosemary bread, which I just made, is delicious.

CARAMELIZED ONION BREAD

Total Time: 4 hours 30 minutes | Prep Time: 30 minutes | Yield: 1 loaf

Ingredients:

1 cup warm water	2 tablespoons olive oil
3 cups bread flour	2 teaspoons sugar
1 1/2 teaspoons salt	2 large onions, thinly sliced
2 tablespoons butter	1 tablespoon brown sugar
2 1/4 teaspoons active dry yeast	

Directions:

(1) While the pan is on medium heat, melt the butter. After about 20 to 25 minutes of stirring occasionally, add the thinly sliced onions and continue cooking until they caramelize. Brown sugar should be stirred in during the final five minutes of cooking. Let sit and cool. *(2)* According to the manufacturer's instructions, put the following ingredients into the bread machine pan: olive oil, warm water, bread flour, sugar, salt, caramelized onions, and active dry yeast. *(3)* To make a 1.5-pound loaf with a color crust of your choice, put your bread machine in Basic or White Bread mode. *(4)* Roll out the bread. *(5)* After the baking time is up, gently take the loaf out of the oven and set it on a wire rack to cool before cutting. *(6)* The Caramelized Onion Bread is ready for your enjoyment.

POTATO BREAD

Total Time: 4 hours | Prep Time: 25 minutes | Yield: 1 loaf

Ingredients:

1 cup warm water	1/2 cup mashed potatoes (cooled)
2 tablespoons butter, softened	3 cups bread flour
2 tablespoons sugar	1 1/2 teaspoons salt
2 1/4 teaspoons active dry yeast	

Directions:

(1) After softening the butter, add the mashed potatoes, warm water, bread flour, sugar, salt, and active dry yeast to the bread machine pan in the sequence specified by the owner. *(2)* To make a 1.5-pound loaf with a color crust of your choice, put your bread machine in Basic or White Bread mode. *(3)* Roll out the bread. *(4)* After the baking time is up, gently take the loaf out of the oven and set it on a wire rack to cool before cutting. *(5)* Potato bread is best enjoyed warm in the oven.

BUTTERMILK BREAD

Total Time: 3 hours 40 minutes | Prep Time: 20 minutes | Yield: 1 loaf

Ingredients:

1 cup warm buttermilk	2 tablespoons butter, melted
3 cups bread flour	2 tablespoons sugar

1 1/2 teaspoons salt   2 1/4 teaspoons active dry yeast

Directions:

(1) As instructed by the manufacturer, bread flour, sugar, salt, and active dried yeast should be added to the receptacle of the bread machine in that order. Additionally, warm buttermilk must be added. **(2)** When you want a loaf that weighs 1.5 pounds and has the crust color you want, you should use the Basic or White Bread setting on your bread machine. **(3)** To begin, turn on the bread machine. **(4)** Before slicing the bread, carefully remove it from the pan once the baking cycle has been completed and allow it to cool on a wire rack. **(5)** Take pleasure in your buttermilk bread that has just been cooked.

PUMPKIN BREAD

Total Time: 4 hours 15 minutes | Prep Time: 30 minutes | Yield: 1 loaf

Ingredients:

1 cup canned pumpkin puree	1/2 cup warm water
2 tablespoons olive oil	3 cups bread flour
1/4 cup brown sugar	1 1/2 teaspoons salt
1 teaspoon ground cinnamon	1/2 teaspoon ground nutmeg
1/4 teaspoon ground cloves	2 1/4 teaspoons active dry yeast

Directions:

(1) Follow the manufacturer-recommended sequence of ingredients in the bread machine pan: pumpkin puree from a can, warm water, olive oil, flour for bread, brown sugar, salt, cinnamon, nutmeg, cloves, and active dry yeast. **(2)** To make a 1.5-pound loaf with a color crust of your choice, put your bread machine in Basic or White Bread mode. **(3)** Roll out the bread. **(4)** After the baking time is up, gently take the loaf out of the oven and set it on a wire rack to cool before cutting. **(5)** Savor the aroma of pumpkin bread baking in the oven.

BANANA NUT BREAD

Total Time: 3 hours 30 minutes | Prep Time: 10 minutes

Ingredients:

3 ripe bananas, mashed	1/2 cup chopped walnuts
2 cups all-purpose flour	1 teaspoon baking soda
1/2 teaspoon salt	1/2 cup unsalted butter, melted
3/4 cup granulated sugar	2 large eggs
1 teaspoon vanilla extract	

Directions:

(1) Your Zojirushi bread maker needs to be preheated. **(2)** Mash the bananas and add the chopped walnuts to a bowl. **(3)** Flour, baking soda, and salt should be mixed in a separate bowl. **(4)** Combine the sugar and melted butter in the receptacle of the bread machine. After adjusting the dial to the "Cake" setting, seal the lid. **(5)** Once the butter and sugar have been incorporated, gradually incorporate the eggs, followed by the vanilla essence. **(6)** While stirring thoroughly after each addition, slowly pour the flour mixture into the bread pan. **(7)** Finally, combine the walnuts and bananas and fold them in. **(8)** Put the lid back on the bread maker and let it finish baking. **(9)** Once the bread has been baked, transfer it to a wire rack to chill entirely prior to dividing.

BLUEBERRY LEMON BREAD

Total Time: 3 hours 45 minutes | Prep Time: 15 minutes

Ingredients:

1 cup fresh blueberries	Zest of 1 lemon
2 cups all-purpose flour	1 teaspoon baking powder
1/2 teaspoon baking soda	1/2 teaspoon salt
1/2 cup unsalted butter, softened	3/4 cup granulated sugar
2 large eggs	1/2 cup plain yogurt
2 tablespoons lemon juice	1 teaspoon vanilla extract

Directions:

(1) Your Zojirushi bread maker needs to be preheated. **(2)** Set aside after tossing the blueberries with the zest of the lemon. **(3)** Combine the salt, baking soda, flour, and baking powder in a bowl and mix well. *(4)* Cream the sugar and softened butter in the bread machine's bread pan until the mixture is light and airy. Find and choose the "Cake" option. *(5)* Gradually add the eggs while whisking constantly. *(6)* Whisk in the unflavored yogurt, squeezed lemon juice, and vanilla essence. *(7)* While stirring thoroughly after each addition, slowly pour the flour mixture into the bread pan. *(8)* The mixture of blueberries and lemon zest should be gently folded in. *(9)* Put the lid back on the bread maker and let it finish baking. *(10)* Once the bread has been baked, transfer it to a wire rack to chill entirely prior to dividing.

CHOCOLATE CHIP BREAD

Total Time: 4 hours | Prep Time: 20 minutes

Ingredients:

1 cup semisweet chocolate chips	2 cups all-purpose flour
1 teaspoon baking soda	1/2 teaspoon salt
1/2 cup unsalted butter, softened	3/4 cup granulated sugar
2 large eggs	1 teaspoon vanilla extract
1 cup milk	

Directions:

(1) Zojirushi bread machine preheat. *(2)* Coat chocolate chips with a spoonful of flour in a bowl. *(3)* Mix the remaining flour, baking soda, and salt in another dish. *(4)* Cream softened butter and sugar in the bread machine pan until frothy. Choose "Cake". *(5)* After adding each egg, mix well, then add the vanilla essence. *(6)* Slowly incorporate the flour mixture into the bread pan while alternating with the milk. Mix thoroughly. *(7)* Mix in chocolate chips. *(8)* Let the bread machine finish baking with the cover closed. *(9)* Once the bread is done, remove it from the pan with care and allow it to settle on a wire stand prior to slicing.

CRANBERRY ORANGE BREAD

Total Time: 3 hours 45 minutes | Prep Time: 15 minutes

Ingredients:

1 cup dried cranberries	Zest of 1 orange
2 cups all-purpose flour	1 teaspoon baking powder
1/2 teaspoon baking soda	1/2 teaspoon salt
1/2 cup unsalted butter, softened	3/4 cup granulated sugar
2 large eggs	1/2 cup orange juice
1 teaspoon vanilla extract	

Directions:

(1) Zojirushi bread machine preheat. *(2)* Mix orange zest with dried cranberries and set aside. *(3)* Mix flour, baking powder, soda, and salt in a bowl. *(4)* Cream softened butter and sugar in the bread machine pan until frothy. Choose "Cake". *(5)* After adding each egg, mix well. *(6)* Add orange juice and vanilla. *(7)* While stirring constantly, gradually pour the flour mixture into the bread pan. *(8)* The cranberry-orange zest mixture should be gently folded in. *(9)* Let the bread machine finish baking with the cover closed. *(10)* After the bread has been baked, carefully place it on a wire rack to cool. Then, slice it.

ZUCCHINI BREAD

Total Time: 3 hours 30 minutes | Prep Time: 10 minutes

Ingredients:

1 cup grated zucchini	1/2 cup chopped walnuts
2 cups all-purpose flour	1 teaspoon baking powder
1/2 teaspoon baking soda	1/2 teaspoon salt
1 teaspoon ground cinnamon	1/4 teaspoon ground nutmeg
1/2 cup unsalted butter, softened	3/4 cup granulated sugar
2 large eggs	1 teaspoon vanilla extract

Directions:

(1) Set your Zojirushi bread maker to preheat. *(2)* Add the chopped walnuts and the grated zucchini to a bowl. *(3)* In another dish, whisk together the flour, baking powder, baking soda, salt, cinnamon, and nutmeg. *(4)* Beat the sugar

and softened butter in the bread pan of the bread maker until they are light and fluffy. Choose the "Cake" configuration. *(5)* Stir in the vanilla extract last, and then add the eggs one at a time, mixing well after each addition. *(6)* Allowing each addition to thoroughly mix, add the flour mixture to the bread pan one at a time. *(7)* Stir in the mixture of walnuts and zucchini. *(8)* Let the bread machine finish its baking cycle by closing the lid. *(9)* When the bread is finished, carefully take it out of the pan and allow it to cool on a wire rack before slicing.

CARROT CAKE BREAD

Total Time: 3 hours 30 minutes | Prep Time: 15 minutes | Yield: 1 loaf

Ingredients:

1 cup grated carrots	1/2 cup raisins
1/2 cup chopped walnuts	2 tablespoons honey
1 teaspoon ground cinnamon	1/4 teaspoon ground nutmeg
1/4 teaspoon ground ginger	1/4 teaspoon salt
2 cups bread flour	2 teaspoons active dry yeast

Directions:

(1) Garlic that has been grated, raisins, chopped walnuts, honey, cinnamon, nutmeg, ginger, and salt should be mixed together in the pan of the bread machine. *(2)* In addition to the carrot mixture, sprinkle bread flour on top. *(3)* After creating a small well in the middle of the flour, add the yeast to the mixture. *(4)* Choose either the "Basic" or "White Bread" setting on the bread machine after you have inserted the bread pan into the machine. *(5)* Set the bread machine to dough-making mode. After the bread has been baked, remove it from the machine and set it on a wire rack to cool before cutting.

ARTICHOKE AND PARMESAN BREAD

Total Time: 3 hours 45 minutes | Prep Time: 20 minutes | Yield: 1 loaf

Ingredients:

one cup of marinated artichoke hearts, drained and chopped	1/2 cup grated Parmesan cheese
2 tablespoons chopped fresh basil	1 tablespoon olive oil
1 teaspoon garlic powder	1/4 teaspoon black pepper
2 cups bread flour	2 teaspoons active dry yeast

Directions:

(1) Grated Parmesan cheese, chopped fresh basil, olive oil, black pepper, and garlic powder should all be combined in the bread maker pan. *(2)* Sprinkle the artichoke mixture with bread flour. *(3)* In the center of the flour, create a tiny well and add the yeast. *(4)* After placing the bread pan inside the bread maker, choose the "Dough" setting. *(5)* Take the dough out of the machine after the dough cycle is finished, then form it into a loaf. *(6)* For about 45 minutes, the dough should rise in a warm location after being placed in a loaf pan that has been oiled and covered with a fresh kitchen towel. *(7)* Set oven temperature to 175°C. The bread should bake for 30 to 35 minutes or until golden brown. Take it out of the oven, allow it to cool, and then slice.

MAPLE PECAN BREAD

Total Time: 3 hours 15 minutes | Prep Time: 15 minutes | Yield: 1 loaf

Ingredients:

1/2 cup chopped pecans	2 tablespoons maple syrup
2 tablespoons unsalted butter, melted	1/4 teaspoon salt
2 cups bread flour	2 teaspoons active dry yeast
1/2 cup milk	1/4 cup water

Directions:

(1) In a small bowl, mix chopped pecans, maple syrup, melted butter, and salt. Save. *(2)* Mix flour and active dry yeast in the bread machine pan. *(3)* Cook milk and water in a microwave-safe bowl until warm (110°F or 45°C). *(4)* Add warm milk to the bread machine pan. *(5)* Start the breadmaker on "Dough". The dough should be removed from the machine after the cycle. *(6)* On a surface dusted with flour, roll out the dough to form a rectangle. Scatter the pecan mixture evenly over the dough. *(7)* Pinch the seams

closed to seal the dough as you roll it tightly, beginning with the longest edge. *(8)* Wrap the dough in a clean kitchen towel and set it aside to rise in a warm place for 45 minutes after transferring it to an oiled loaf pan. *(9)* Preheat oven to 375°F (190°C). Bake bread till golden brown, 25-30 minutes. Slice after cooling from the oven.

ALMOND CHERRY BREAD

Total Time: 3 hours 45 minutes | Prep Time: 15 minutes | Yield: 1 loaf

Ingredients:

1/2 cup dried cherries, chopped	1/2 cup sliced almonds
2 tablespoons honey	1/4 teaspoon almond extract
2 cups bread flour	2 teaspoons active dry yeast
3/4 cup warm water	

Directions:

(1) All of the following ingredients should be combined in the pan of the bread machine: chopped dried cherries, sliced almonds, honey, and almond extract. *(2)* It is recommended that bread flour and active dry yeast be added to the cherry mixture. *(3)* The flour should be poured over the warm water. *(4)* After placing the bread pan into the bread machine, choose the "Sweet" or "Fruit & Nut" setting on the bread maker. *(5)* Switch on the bread maker to get started. When the bread is baked, take it out of the machine and let it cool on a wire rack before slicing.

FIG AND WALNUT BREAD

Total Time: 3 hours 30 minutes | Prep Time: 15 minutes | Yield: 1 loaf

Ingredients:

1/2 cup dried figs, chopped	1/2 cup chopped walnuts
2 tablespoons honey	1 teaspoon ground cinnamon
1/4 teaspoon salt	2 cups bread flour
2 teaspoons active dry yeast	3/4 cup warm milk

Directions:

(1) The dried figs, walnuts, honey, cinnamon, and salt should be mixed together in the pan of the bread machine. *(2)* Stir in the active dry yeast and bread flour after combining the fig mixture. *(3)* The flour should be poured over the warm milk. *(4)* Make sure the bread pan is properly inserted into the bread machine, and then choose either the "Basic" or "White Bread" preset. *(5)* Switch on the bread maker to get started. When the bread is baked, take it out of the machine and let it cool on a wire rack before slicing.

APRICOT ALMOND BREAD

Total Time: 3 hours 30 minutes | Prep Time: 15 minutes | Yield: 1 loaf

Ingredients:

1 cup water	3 tablespoons honey
2 tablespoons olive oil	1 teaspoon salt
3 cups bread flour	2 teaspoons active dry yeast
½ cup chopped dried apricots	½ cup chopped almonds

Directions:

(1) As directed by the manufacturer, fill the bread pan of your Zojirushi bread maker with water, honey, olive oil, salt, bread flour, and yeast. *(2)* If you want a 2-pound loaf with a light crust, use your machine's "Basic" or "White Bread" setting. *(3)* When the machine beeps or indicates that more ingredients are needed, add the chopped dried apricots and almonds. *(4)* Shut the cover and allow the bread maker to finish the chosen cycle. *(5)* Before slicing, take the bread pan from the oven with caution and allow it to cool on a wire rack when the baking cycle has finished. Savor the flavor of your apricot almond bread!

DATE AND NUT BREAD

Total Time: 3 hours 45 minutes | Prep Time: 20 minutes | Yield: 1 loaf

Ingredients:

1 ¼ cups warm milk	2 tablespoons unsalted butter, softened
1 teaspoon salt	3 cups bread flour
2 teaspoons active dry yeast	½ cup chopped dates

½ cup chopped mixed nuts (such as walnuts, pecans, or almonds)

Directions:

(1) Prepare the bread flour, yeast, softened butter, warm milk, and salt in the bread pan of your Zojirushi bread maker as directed by the manufacturer. **(2)** To make a 2-pound loaf with a medium crust, use your machine's "Sweet" option. **(3)** The machine will beep or indicate that more ingredients are needed; add the chopped dates and mixed nuts then. **(4)** Shut the bread maker and allow it to finish the chosen cycle. **(5)** At the end of the bread cycle, carefully remove the bread pan from the oven. Prior to slicing, allow it to cool on a wire rack. Cheers to a fantastic night on the town and some delicious nutbread!

PISTACHIO CRANBERRY BREAD

Total Time: 3 hours 30 minutes | Prep Time: 15 minutes | Yield: 1 loaf

Ingredients:

1 cup water	2 tablespoons olive oil
3 tablespoons honey	1 teaspoon salt
3 cups bread flour	2 teaspoons active dry yeast
½ cup shelled pistachios, chopped	½ cup dried cranberries

Directions:

(1) In the bread pan of your Zojirushi bread maker, add water, olive oil, honey, salt, bread flour, and yeast as directed by the manufacturer. **(2)** To achieve a light crust and a 2-pound loaf, use your machine's "Basic" or "White Bread" preset. **(3)** The machine will beep or signal for more ingredients; add the chopped pistachios and dried cranberries then. **(4)** Shut the bread maker's cover and let it finish the chosen cycle. **(5)** Before slicing, let the baking pan cool entirely on a wire rack after taking it out of the oven. The pistachio cranberry bread is best-enjoyed bite by bite.

CINNAMON RAISIN BREAD

Total Time: 3 hours 30 minutes | Prep Time: 15 minutes | Yield: 1 loaf

Ingredients:

1 ¼ cups warm milk	2 tablespoons unsalted butter, softened
1 teaspoon salt	3 cups bread flour
2 teaspoons active dry yeast	½ cup raisins
2 teaspoons ground cinnamon	

Directions:

(1) Following the manufacturer's directions, mix the yeast, bread flour, salt, melted butter, warm milk, and Zojirushi bread machine's bread pan. **(2)** If you want a 2-pound loaf with a medium crust, turn your machine to the "Sweet" setting. **(3)** When the machine beeps or signals for further ingredients, add the ground cinnamon and raisins. **(4)** Allow the bread machine to finish the programmed cycle after you've closed the lid. **(5)** After the baking cycle is complete, carefully take the bread pan out of the machine and let it cool on a wire rack. Then, slice it. I hope you savor this fragrant cinnamon raisin bread.

CARDAMOM BREAD

Total Time: 3 hours 30 minutes | Prep Time: 15 minutes | Yield: 1 loaf

Ingredients:

1 cup water	2 tablespoons unsalted butter, softened
1 teaspoon salt	3 cups bread flour
2 teaspoons active dry yeast	1 tablespoon ground cardamom
Two tablespoons granulated sugar	

Directions:

(1) Make sure to follow the manufacturer's directions for your Zojirushi bread machine while placing the following ingredients into the bread pan: water, melted butter, salt, bread flour, yeast, ground cardamom, and granulated sugar. **(2)** If you want a 2-pound loaf with a thin crust, turn your bread machine to the "Basic" or "White Bread" preset. **(3)** Allow the bread machine to finish the programmed cycle after you've closed the lid. **(4)** Carefully take the bread pan out of the oven when the baking cycle is finished. Place it on a wire rack to cool before slicing. Hope you savor the aromatic cardamom bread!

COCONUT BREAD

Total Time: 3 hours 30 minutes | Prep Time: 15 minutes

Ingredients:

1 cup coconut milk	2 tablespoons coconut oil, melted
3 cups bread flour	2 tablespoons sugar
1 teaspoon salt	2 teaspoons active dry yeast
1/2 cup shredded coconut	

Directions:

(1) Melt coconut oil and mix coconut milk in the bread machine pan. *(2)* Over the liquid components in the pan, add bread flour, sugar, salt, and yeast. *(3)* Set your bread machine to basic white bread for a 2-pound loaf and start it. *(4)* Scrape the dough from the machine and mix in the shredded coconut until equally distributed. *(5)* Shape the dough into a loaf and grease a pan. *(6)* Permit to continue rising for one another hour in a warm area, after which cover with a clean dish towel and let it double in size. *(7)* Set oven temperature to 350°F. *(8)* The bread should be hollow when tapped underneath and golden brown after 30 to 35 minutes of baking. *(9)* After 10 minutes, take the bread out of the pan and set it on a wire rack to cool entirely.

NUTELLA SWIRL BREAD

Total Time: 3 hours 45 minutes | Prep Time: 20 minutes

Ingredients:

1 cup whole milk	2 tablespoons unsalted butter, softened
3 cups bread flour	2 tablespoons sugar
1 teaspoon salt	2 teaspoons active dry yeast
1/2 cup Nutella	

Directions:

(1) Pour warm whole milk into the bread machine pan. *(2)* Put softened butter, bread flour, sugar, salt, and yeast in the milk in the pan. *(3)*

Select the bread machine dough cycle and start it. *(4)* After taking the dough out of the machine, roll it out into a rectangle on a surface dusted with flour. Spread Nutella over the dough evenly. *(5)* To form a loaf, begin rolling the dough tightly from the long edge. Seam-side down, place dough in an oiled loaf pan. *(6)* Permit to continue rising for one another hour in a warm area, after which cover with a clean dish towel and let it double in size. *(7)* Heat the oven to 190°C. *(8)* The bread should be golden brown and hollow when tapped after 25–30 minutes. *(9)* Before moving the bread onto a wire rack, let it cool in the pan for ten minutes.

CHAI SPICE BREAD

Total Time: 4 hours | Prep Time: 25 minutes

Ingredients:

1 cup strong brewed chai tea, cooled	2 tablespoons honey
3 cups bread flour	2 tablespoons sugar
1 teaspoon salt	2 teaspoons active dry yeast
1 teaspoon ground cinnamon	1/2 teaspoon ground ginger
1/4 teaspoon ground cardamom	1/4 teaspoon ground cloves

Directions:

(1) Chilled chai tea and honey in the bread machine pan. *(2)* Over the liquid components in the pan, add bread flour, sugar, salt, yeast, cinnamon, ginger, cardamom, and cloves. *(3)* For a 2-pound loaf, start your bread maker on basic white bread. *(4)* Scrape the dough from the machine and form it into a loaf. *(5)* Fill a greased loaf pan with dough. *(6)* The dough needs an hour to double in size when left to rise in a warm spot, covered with a clean kitchen towel. *(7)* Start with a 350°F (175°C) oven. *(8)* The bread needs to be a golden brown color and hollow when tapped after 30–35 minutes in the oven. *(9)* Before moving the bread to a wire rack, let it cool for 10 minutes in the pan.

BEER BREAD

Total Time: 3 hours 45 minutes | Prep Time: 15 minutes

Ingredients:

1 cup beer, room temperature	2 tablespoons honey
3 cups bread flour	1 teaspoon salt
2 teaspoons active dry yeast	

Directions:

(1) Fill the bread machine pan with beer and honey. (2) Top the liquid ingredients in the pan with bread flour, salt, and yeast. (3) Start your bread machine with the basic white bread setting for a 2-pound loaf. (4) Remove the dough from the machine and form it into a loaf. (5) Grease and place the dough in a loaf pan. (6) To ensure that it doubles in size, place the pan in a warm place and cover it with a fresh kitchen towel. (7) 190°C is the oven temperature. (8) In around 30 to 35 minutes, the bread should be hollow to the touch and golden brown. (9) Take the bread out of the pan and let it cool for ten minutes after placing it on a wire rack.

PRETZEL BREAD

Total Time: 4 hours 30 minutes | Prep Time: 30 minutes

Ingredients:

1 cup warm water	2 tablespoons unsalted butter, melted
3 cups bread flour	2 tablespoons brown sugar
1 teaspoon salt	2 teaspoons active dry yeast
1/4 cup baking soda	Coarse salt for topping

Directions:

(1) Butter and warm water in the bread machine pan. (2) Put bread flour, brown sugar, salt, and yeast over the liquid in the pan. (3) Start the bread machine dough cycle. (4) Remove the dough from the machine and split it into equal rolls or loaves. (5) Leave space between dough pieces on a parchment-lined baking pan. (6) Let the dough rise in a warm place for an hour until doubled under a clean kitchen towel. (7) Preheat oven to 375°F (190°C). (8) Add baking soda to boiling water in a large pot. (9) Carefully place risen dough pieces in boiling water for 30 seconds on each side. (10) Before transferring the dough pieces to the baking sheet, use a

slotted spoon to take them from the water. Sprinkle coarse salt over the dough's surface. (11) Bread should be golden brown after 20–25 minutes. (12) Cool bread on a wire rack before serving. Enjoy homemade pretzel bread!

PIZZA DOUGH

Total Time: 2 hours 30 minutes | Prep Time: 10 minutes

Ingredients:

1 cup warm water	2 tablespoons olive oil
3 cups bread flour	1 teaspoon sugar
1 teaspoon salt	2 1/4 teaspoons active dry yeast
1 teaspoon Italian seasoning (optional)	

Directions:

(1) Warm water, olive oil, bread flour, sugar, salt, and Italian seasoning should all be combined in the bread machine pan. (2) Create a tiny indentation in the middle of the flour mixture and incorporate the yeast. (3) After placing the bread pan into the bread maker, choose the "Dough" cycle. (4) After the cycle is finished, take the dough out of the machine and transfer it to a surface dusted with flour. (5) A temperature of 220°C should be set for the oven. Roll out the dough into two equal sections, each forming a circle. (6) After putting the dough rounds on pizza pans that have been greased, give them ten minutes to rest. (7) Once the dough has rested, cover it with your preferred pizza toppings. (8) Roast in a preheated oven for fifteen to twenty minutes to get the crust golden brown and the toppings cooked to your preference. Serve warm after chopping.

FOCACCIA BREAD

Total Time: 3 hours | Prep Time: 15 minutes

Ingredients:

1 1/4 cups warm water	3 tablespoons olive oil, divided
3 cups bread flour	1 teaspoon sugar
1 teaspoon salt	2 1/4 teaspoons active dry yeast
1 tablespoon fresh rosemary, chopped	Coarse sea salt for sprinkling

Directions:

(1) In the bread machine pan, mix warm water, 2 tablespoons olive oil, flour, sugar, salt, and yeast. (2) Before starting the bread machine, place the pan inside and select "Dough." (3) Put the dough in a greased bowl after the cycle. (4) A clean kitchen towel should cover the bowl, and let the dough rest in a warm area for an hour until doubled. (5) Preheat oven to 400°F (200°C). (6) Punch down and place the dough on a prepared baking sheet. (7) Press dough into a 1-inch-thick rectangle. (8) Make dough indentations using your fingertips. (9) Finally, drizzle the dough with the last tablespoon of olive oil. (10) Cover the dough with chopped rosemary and coarse sea salt. (11) After 20–25 minutes in the preheated oven, the focaccia should be golden brown and hollow when tapped. (12) Before slicing and serving, let focaccia cool.

OLIVE OIL BREAD

Total Time: 4 hours | Prep Time: 20 minutes

Ingredients:

1 1/2 cups warm water	1/4 cup olive oil
4 cups bread flour	2 tablespoons sugar
1 1/2 teaspoons salt	2 1/4 teaspoons active dry yeast
2 tablespoons dried oregano	1 tablespoon dried basil

Directions:

(1) In the bread machine pan, mix warm water, olive oil, flour, sugar, salt, yeast, dried oregano, and basil. (2) In the bread maker, place the bread pan and select "Dough." Put the dough in a greased bowl after the cycle. (3) The dough needs an hour to double in size when it's warmed and covered with a clean kitchen towel. (4) Preheat oven to 375°F (190°C). (5) Punch down and loosen the dough. (6) Loosely place the dough in an oiled loaf pan and cover with plastic wrap. The dough should rise for 30–45 minutes, just over the loaf pan. (7) Bake the bread for 30–35 minutes in the preheated oven until golden brown and hollow when tapped. (8) The bread should be removed from the pan after 10 minutes and left to cool entirely on a wire rack.

ONION DILL BREAD

Total Time: 3 hours 30 minutes | Prep Time: 15 minutes

Ingredients:

1 1/4 cups warm water	2 tablespoons olive oil
3 cups bread flour	1 tablespoon sugar
1 1/2 teaspoons salt	2 1/4 teaspoons active dry yeast
1/4 cup dried minced onion	2 tablespoons dried dill weed

Directions:

(1) Place warm water, olive oil, bread flour, sugar, salt, yeast, dried chopped onion, and dried dill weed in the bread machine pan. (2) Insert the bread pan and choose "Dough" in the bread machine. (3) Transfer the dough to a greased basin after the cycle. (4) A clean kitchen towel should cover the bowl, and let the dough rest in a warm place for 1-2 hours until doubled. (5) Make sure your oven is 375°F (190°C). (6) Work the dough into a loaf. (7) Layer plastic wrap loosely over the dough in a greased loaf pan. (8) Continue rising the dough for 30–45 minutes until it just touches the loaf pan. (9) Bake for thirty to thirty-five minutes or until the bread is hollow when tapped and golden brown. (10) After ten minutes of taking the bread out of the pan, set it on a wire rack to cool entirely.

ASIAGO CHEESE BREAD

Total Time: 3 hours 15 minutes | Prep Time: 15 minutes

Ingredients:

1 1/4 cups warm water	2 tablespoons olive oil
3 cups bread flour	1 tablespoon sugar
1 1/2 teaspoons salt	2 1/4 teaspoons active dry yeast
1 cup shredded Asiago cheese	

Directions:

(1) In the bread machine pan, mix warm water, olive oil, flour, sugar, salt, yeast, and Asiago cheese. (2) In the bread maker, place the bread pan and select "Dough." Put the dough in a greased bowl after the cycle. (3) The dough needs at least an hour, or until it has doubled in size, to rise in a warm place, covered with a clean

kitchen towel. **(4)** Preheat oven to 375°F (190°C). **(5)** Punch down and loosen the dough. **(6)** Loosely place the dough in an oiled loaf pan and cover with plastic wrap. The dough should rise for 30–45 minutes, just over the loaf pan. **(7)** Bake the bread for 30–35 minutes in the preheated oven until golden brown and hollow when tapped. **(8)** The bread should be removed from the pan after 10 minutes and left to cool entirely on a wire rack.

PARMESAN HERB BREADSTICKS

Total Time: 2 hours 30 minutes | Prep Time: 15 minutes | Yield: 12 breadsticks

Ingredients:

1 cup warm water	2 tablespoons olive oil
3 cups bread flour	2 tablespoons grated Parmesan cheese
1 tablespoon sugar	1 teaspoon salt
1 teaspoon dried basil	1 teaspoon dried oregano
1 teaspoon garlic powder	2 1/4 teaspoons active dry yeast

Directions:

(1) Following the manufacturer's recommendations, put warm water, olive oil, bread flour, Parmesan cheese, sugar, salt, basil, oregano, garlic powder, and yeast in the bread machine pan. **(2)** Press start after selecting the dough cycle. **(3)** Move the dough to a surface that has been lightly floured after the dough cycle is finished. **(4)** Set oven temperature to 190°C. **(5)** Roll each of the twelve equal amounts of dough into a breadstick form. **(6)** Put the breadsticks on a baking sheet that has been oiled, cover them with a fresh cloth, and allow them to rise for half an hour in a warm location. **(7)** Bake for 15-20 minutes, or until golden brown, in an oven that has been warmed. **(8)** Enjoy while warm!

PIZZA ROLLS

Total Time: 3 hours | Prep Time: 20 minutes | Yield: 12 rolls

Ingredients:

1 cup warm water	2 tablespoons olive oil
3 cups bread flour	1 tablespoon sugar
1 teaspoon salt	1 teaspoon garlic powder
2 1/4 teaspoons active dry yeast	1/2 cup pizza sauce
1 cup shredded mozzarella cheese	1/4 cup sliced pepperoni
1/4 cup diced bell peppers	1/4 cup sliced black olives

Directions:

(1) In the bread machine pan, add warm water, olive oil, bread flour, sugar, salt, garlic powder, and yeast in the manufacturer's sequence. **(2)** Choose the dough cycle and start. **(3)** Place the dough on a lightly floured surface after the dough cycle. **(4)** Preheat oven to 375°F (190°C). **(5)** Roll dough into a 1/4-inch rectangle. **(6)** Spread pizza sauce on dough, leaving a small border. **(7)** Add pepperoni, bell peppers, and black olives to the sauce with mozzarella cheese. **(8)** Roll dough tightly from one long edge. **(9)** Place 12 equal slices of rolled dough on a prepared baking sheet. **(10)** Let rise for 30 minutes in a warm location under a clean cloth. **(11)** Bake 20–25 minutes in preheated oven till golden brown. **(12)** Warm with extra pizza sauce for dipping.

SPINACH AND CHEESE ROLLS

Total Time: 3 hours 30 minutes | Prep Time: 25 minutes | Yield: 12 rolls

Ingredients:

1 cup warm water	2 tablespoons olive oil
3 cups bread flour	1 tablespoon sugar
1 teaspoon salt	1 teaspoon garlic powder
2 1/4 teaspoons active dry yeast	1 cup chopped fresh spinach
1 cup shredded mozzarella cheese	1/2 cup grated Parmesan cheese
1/4 cup finely chopped onion	1/4 cup chopped sun-dried tomatoes

Directions:

(1) In the bread machine pan, add warm water, olive oil, bread flour, sugar, salt, garlic powder, and yeast in the manufacturer's sequence. **(2)** Choose the dough cycle and start. **(3)** Place the dough on a lightly floured surface after the dough cycle. **(4)** Preheat oven to 375°F (190°C). **(5)** Roll dough into a 1/4-inch rectangle. **(6)** Evenly sprinkle chopped spinach, mozzarella,

Parmesan, onion, and sun-dried tomatoes on the dough. *(7)* Roll dough tightly from one long edge. *(8)* Place 12 equal slices of rolled dough on a prepared baking sheet. *(9)* Let rise for 30 minutes in a warm location under a clean cloth. *(10)* Bake 20–25 minutes in preheated oven till golden brown. *(11)* Serve hot and relish!

CINNAMON ROLLS

Total Time: 4 hours | Prep Time: 30 minutes | Yield: 12 rolls

Ingredients:

1 cup warm milk	2 eggs
1/3 cup melted butter	4 1/2 cups bread flour
1/2 cup white sugar	2 1/4 teaspoons active dry yeast
1 teaspoon salt	1/2 cup packed brown sugar
2 1/2 tablespoons ground cinnamon	1/3 cup softened butter
1 1/2 cups confectioners' sugar	3 tablespoons milk
1 teaspoon vanilla extract	

Directions:

(1) Follow the manufacturer's sequence for warm milk, eggs, melted butter, bread flour, white sugar, yeast, and salt in the bread machine pan. *(2)* Choose the dough cycle and start. *(3)* Place the dough on a lightly floured surface after the dough cycle. *(4)* Preheat oven to 375°F (190°C). *(5)* Large, 1/4-inch-thick rectangle of dough. *(6)* Put cinnamon and brown sugar in a small bowl and mix. Sprinkle cinnamon-sugar mixture over softened butter on dough. *(7)* Roll dough tightly from one long edge. *(8)* Place 12 equal slices of rolled dough on a prepared baking sheet. *(9)* Let rise for 30 minutes in a warm location under a clean cloth. *(10)* Bake 20–25 minutes in preheated oven till golden brown. *(11)* Make the glaze by whisking confectioners' sugar, milk, and vanilla extract in a small bowl. *(12)* Pour glaze over warm cinnamon buns and serve.

RASPBERRY ALMOND ROLLS

Total Time: 4 hours 30 minutes | Prep Time: 35 minutes | Yield: 12 rolls

Ingredients:

1 cup warm milk	2 eggs
1/3 cup melted butter	4 1/2 cups bread flour
1/2 cup white sugar	2 1/4 teaspoons active dry yeast
1 teaspoon salt	1 cup raspberry jam
1/2 cup sliced almonds	1 1/2 cups confectioners' sugar
3 tablespoons milk	1 teaspoon almond extract

Directions:

(1) Follow the manufacturer's sequence for warm milk, eggs, melted butter, bread flour, white sugar, yeast, and salt in the bread machine pan. *(2)* Choose the dough cycle and start. *(3)* Place the dough on a lightly floured surface after the dough cycle. *(4)* Preheat oven to 375°F (190°C). *(5)* Large, 1/4-inch-thick rectangle of dough. *(6)* Sprinkle sliced almonds over raspberry jam-covered dough. *(7)* Roll dough tightly from one long edge. *(8)* Place 12 equal slices of rolled dough on a prepared baking sheet. *(9)* Let rise for 30 minutes in a warm location under a clean cloth. *(10)* Bake 20–25 minutes in preheated oven till golden brown. *(11)* To make the glaze, divide the milk among two bowls and combine it with the confectioners' sugar and almond essence. *(12)* Pour glaze over heated raspberry almond buns and serve.

LEMON CREAM CHEESE ROLLS

Total Time: 3 hours 30 minutes | Prep Time: 30 minutes | Yields: 12 rolls

Ingredients:

1 cup warm milk (110°F)	1/4 cup granulated sugar
2 1/4 teaspoons active dry yeast	1/4 cup unsalted butter, melted
1 teaspoon salt	2 large eggs
4 cups all-purpose flour	8 oz cream cheese, softened
1/3 cup powdered sugar	Zest of 2 lemons

1/4 cup lemon juice

1 tablespoon lemon zest (for filling)

1/4 cup granulated sugar (for filling)

Directions:

(1) Warm milk, granulated sugar, and yeast in the bread machine pan. Wait 5 minutes for foam. **(2)** Put the melted butter, salt, eggs, and flour in the pan. Select the dough cycle and begin. **(3)** Cream cheese, powdered sugar, lemon zest, and juice should be mixed until smooth in a bowl. Set aside. **(4)** After the dough cycle, turn it out onto a floured surface. Roll into a 16x12-inch rectangle. **(5)** Dot the dough with the cream cheese mixture, ensuring a 1/2-inch border around the edges. Grated sugar and lemon zest should be added. **(6)** Roll the dough tightly from the long side and pinch the seam to seal. Cut 12 equal pieces. **(7)** In a greased 9-by-13-inch pan, lay out the rolls. After an hour of rising in a warm spot, cover it with a clean dish towel. **(8)** Preheating the oven to 175 degrees Celsius is required. After 25-30 minutes, the rolls need to be a golden brown color. **(9)** Serve the rolls after cooling slightly. Savor warm!

ORANGE CRANBERRY ROLLS

Total Time: 3 hours 45 minutes | Prep Time: 45 minutes | Yields: 12 rolls

Ingredients:

1 cup warm orange juice	1/4 cup granulated sugar
2 1/4 teaspoons active dry yeast	1/4 cup unsalted butter, melted
1 teaspoon salt	2 large eggs
4 cups all-purpose flour	1 cup dried cranberries
1/2 cup orange marmalade	1/4 cup powdered sugar (for glaze)
1 tablespoon orange zest (for glaze)	1 tablespoon orange juice (for glaze)

Directions:

(1) Mix yeast, granulated sugar, and warm orange juice in the bread machine pan. Set aside for 5 minutes to foam. **(2)** Pan-add melted butter, salt, eggs, and flour. Select and start the dough cycle. **(3)** Mix in dried cranberries in the last 5 minutes of the dough cycle. **(4)** Turn the dough onto a floured surface after the dough cycle. Roll into a 16x12-inch rectangle. **(5)** Cover the dough with orange marmalade. Roll and pinch the dough to seal. Cut evenly into 12. **(6)** Grease a 9x13-inch pan and place rolls. Rest in a warm place for one hour after covering with a clean dish towel. **(7)** Preheating the oven to 175°C is required. The rolls should be baked for 25 to 30 minutes or until they get a golden color. **(8)** Mix the powdered sugar, orange zest, and juice in a small dish to make the glaze. Drizzle some heated bread on top.

CHOCOLATE HAZELNUT ROLLS

Total Time: 3 hours 30 minutes | Prep Time: 30 minutes

Ingredients:

1 cup milk	1/4 cup unsalted butter, softened
1/4 cup granulated sugar	1 teaspoon salt
3 cups bread flour	2 1/4 teaspoons active dry yeast
1/2 cup chocolate hazelnut spread	1/2 cup chopped hazelnuts
1/4 cup chocolate chips	

Directions:

(1) In the bread machine pan, mix milk softened butter, sugar, salt, flour, and yeast. Switch to the dough and start the machine. **(2)** Once ready, split the dough into 12 equal pieces on a floured surface. Roll each piece into balls. **(3)** Lay each ball out in a circle, add a teaspoon of chocolate hazelnut spread, and top with chopped hazelnuts and chocolate chips. **(4)** Roll and seal each circle into a cylinder. **(5)** When the rolls have risen for an hour in a warm spot, cover them with a clean dish towel and let them double in size. **(6)** Preheat oven to 375°F (190°C). Bake rolls till golden brown, 15-20 minutes. **(7)** After baking, let cool before serving. Warm-up!

SAVORY HERB ROLLS

Total Time: 3 hours 45 minutes | Prep Time: 45 minutes

Ingredients:

1 cup warm water	2 tablespoons olive oil
2 tablespoons granulated sugar	1 teaspoon salt
3 cups bread flour	2 1/4 teaspoons active dry yeast
2 tablespoons chopped fresh herbs	1/4 cup grated Parmesan cheese

Directions:

(1) Warm water, olive oil, sugar, salt, bread flour, and yeast should all be combined in the bread machine pan. Once the dough setting is chosen, turn on the machine. *(2)* When the dough is finished, turn it out onto a surface dusted with flour and work your way into evenly distributing the grated Parmesan cheese and chopped herbs. *(3)* Separate the dough into 12 equal halves. Form a ball with every piece. *(4)* After putting the balls on a baking sheet that has been oiled and covering them with a fresh kitchen towel, let them rise in a warm location for approximately one hour or until they have doubled in size. *(5)* Set oven temperature to 190°C. The rolls should bake for 15 to 20 minutes or until golden brown. *(6)* Before serving, remove it from the oven and allow it to cool slightly. These tasty herb rolls go well with your favorite recipes!

CHEDDAR BACON ROLLS

Total Time: 4 hours | Prep Time: 1 hour

Ingredients:

1 cup warm milk	1/4 cup unsalted butter, melted
2 tablespoons granulated sugar	1 teaspoon salt
3 cups bread flour	2 1/4 teaspoons active dry yeast
1 cup shredded cheddar cheese	1/2 cup cooked and crumbled bacon

Directions:

(1) Warm milk, melted butter, sugar, salt, bread flour, and yeast should all be combined in the bread machine pan. After choosing the dough setting, turn on the machine. *(2)* Incorporate the crumbled bacon and shredded cheddar cheese until thoroughly incorporated after turning the dough out onto a surface sprinkled with flour. *(3)* Pinch off a quarter of the dough and divide it into twelve equal portions. *(4)* It should take about an

hour for the balls to double in size after you put them on an oiled baking sheet and cover them with a clean dish towel. *(5)* Set the oven temperature to 190°C. After 20–25 minutes in the oven, the rolls should be golden brown and cooked through. *(6)* Take it out of the oven and allow it to cool down a little before serving. These bacon rolls with cheese are the ideal snack for brunch, breakfast, or any time of day!

HAM AND SWISS ROLLS

Total Time: 3 hours 30 minutes | Prep Time: 15 minutes | Yield: 12 rolls

Ingredients:

1 cup warm water (110°F)	2 tablespoons olive oil
3 cups bread flour	2 tablespoons sugar
1 teaspoon salt	2 1/4 teaspoons active dry yeast
1/2 cup diced ham	1/2 cup shredded Swiss cheese

Directions:

(1) According to the manufacturer, mix warm water, olive oil, bread flour, sugar, salt, and yeast in the bread machine pan. *(2)* Choose the dough cycle and start. *(3)* Place the dough on a lightly floured board after the bread machine dough cycle. Be patient for 10 minutes. *(4)* Form a 12x18-inch rectangle from the dough. *(5)* Cover the dough with chopped ham and grated Swiss cheese. *(6)* Roll the dough into a log from one of the longer sides. *(7)* Put 12 equal log slices in a greased 9x13 baking dish. *(8)* After the rolls have doubled in size, which should take around 45 to 60 minutes, cover them with a clean kitchen towel and lay them away in a warm location. *(9)* Heat oven to 375°F (190°C). *(10)* The rolls should be golden brown after 20–25 minutes in the preheated oven. *(11)* Warm up and enjoy.

SUN-DRIED TOMATO PESTO ROLLS

Total Time: 3 hours 45 minutes | Prep Time: 20 minutes | Yield: 12 rolls

Ingredients:

1 cup warm milk (110°F)	2 tablespoons olive oil
3 cups bread flour	2 tablespoons sugar

1 teaspoon salt	2 1/4 teaspoons active dry yeast
1/4 cup sun-dried tomatoes, chopped	1/4 cup prepared pesto

Directions:

(1) The manufacturer's instructions call for warm milk, olive oil, bread flour, sugar, salt, and yeast in the bread machine pan. *(2)* Choose the dough cycle and start. *(3)* Place the dough on a lightly floured board after the bread machine dough cycle. Be patient for 10 minutes. *(4)* Form a 12x18-inch rectangle from the dough. *(5)* Distribute chopped sun-dried tomatoes and pesto over dough. *(6)* Roll the dough into a log from one of the longer sides. *(7)* Put 12 equal log slices in a greased 9x13 baking dish. *(8)* Leave in a warm place, covered with a clean kitchen towel, until the rolls have doubled in size, around 45 to 60 minutes. *(9)* Heat oven to 375°F (190°C). *(10)* The rolls should be golden brown after 20–25 minutes in the preheated oven. *(11)* Warm up and enjoy.

ROSEMARY OLIVE ROLLS

Total Time: 4 hours | Prep Time: 25 minutes | Yield: 12 rolls

Ingredients:

1 cup warm water (110°F)	2 tablespoons olive oil
3 cups bread flour	2 tablespoons sugar
1 teaspoon salt	2 1/4 teaspoons active dry yeast
1/4 cup chopped Kalamata olives	1 tablespoon chopped fresh rosemary

Directions:

(1) According to the manufacturer, mix warm water, olive oil, bread flour, sugar, salt, and yeast in the bread machine pan. *(2)* Choose the dough cycle and start. *(3)* Place the dough on a lightly floured board after the bread machine dough cycle. Be patient for 10 minutes. *(4)* Form a 12x18-inch rectangle from the dough. *(5)* Cover the dough with chopped olives and fresh rosemary. *(6)* Roll the dough into a log from one of the longer sides. *(7)* Put 12 equal log slices in a greased 9x13 baking dish. *(8)* The rolls need 45

to 60 minutes to double in size when placed in a warm place covered with a clean kitchen towel. *(9)* Heat oven to 375°F (190°C). *(10)* The rolls should be golden brown after 20–25 minutes in the preheated oven. *(11)* Warm up and enjoy.

ASIAGO GARLIC ROLLS

Total Time: 3 hours 45 minutes | Prep Time: 20 minutes | Yield: 12 rolls

Ingredients:

1 cup warm milk (110°F)	2 tablespoons olive oil
3 cups bread flour	2 tablespoons sugar
1 teaspoon salt	2 1/4 teaspoons active dry yeast
1/2 cup shredded Asiago cheese	2 cloves garlic, minced
1 tablespoon chopped fresh parsley	

Directions:

(1) The manufacturer's instructions call for warm milk, olive oil, bread flour, sugar, salt, and yeast in the bread machine pan. *(2)* Choose the dough cycle and start. *(3)* Place the dough on a lightly floured board after the bread machine dough cycle. Be patient for 10 minutes. *(4)* Form a 12x18-inch rectangle from the dough. *(5)* On the dough, evenly distribute shredded Asiago, minced garlic, and chopped parsley. *(6)* Roll the dough into a log from one of the longer sides. *(7)* Put 12 equal log slices in a greased 9x13 baking dish. *(8)* The rolls need 45 to 60 minutes to double in size when placed in a warm place covered with a clean kitchen towel. Heat oven to 375°F (190°C). *(9)* The rolls should be golden brown after 20–25 minutes in the preheated oven. *(10)* Warm up and enjoy.

GARLIC PARMESAN KNOTS

Total Time: 3 hours 45 minutes | Prep Time: 20 minutes | Yield: 12 rolls

Ingredients:

1 cup warm water (110°F)	2 tablespoons olive oil
3 cups bread flour	2 tablespoons sugar

1 teaspoon salt	2 1/4 teaspoons active dry yeast
3 cloves garlic, minced	1/4 cup grated Parmesan cheese
2 tablespoons chopped fresh parsley	

Directions:

(1) The manufacturer's instructions call for warm water, olive oil, bread flour, sugar, salt, and yeast in the bread machine pan. **(2)** Start the dough cycle. **(3)** Put the dough on a lightly floured board after the bread machine cycle. Do nothing for 10 minutes. **(4)** Make a 12x18-inch dough rectangle. **(5)** In a small bowl, mix minced garlic, Parmesan, and parsley. **(6)** Mix garlic, Parmesan, and parsley and sprinkle over dough. **(7)** Dough into 12 strips. **(8)** Knot each strip and place it on a greased baking sheet or sheet. **(9)** In 45-60 minutes, after covering the knots with a clean kitchen towel, they will double in size. **(10)** Prepare the oven at 375°F (190°C). **(11)** Bake the knots till golden brown in the preheated oven for 20–25 minutes. **(12)** Enjoy warm!

APPLE FRITTER BREAD

Total Time: 3 hours 30 minutes | Prep Time: 20 minutes | Yield: 1 loaf

Ingredients:

1 cup warm water	2 tablespoons butter, softened
3 cups bread flour	3 tablespoons sugar
1 1/2 teaspoons salt	1 teaspoon ground cinnamon
2 teaspoons active dry yeast	1 cup diced apples
1/2 cup chopped pecans	1/4 cup brown sugar
1 teaspoon ground cinnamon	1/4 cup powdered sugar
1 tablespoon milk	

Directions:

(1) Warm water, butter, bread flour, sugar, salt, cinnamon, and yeast should be in the bread machine pan in the manufacturer's order. **(2)** Pick the dough cycle and start it. **(3)** The dough should be transferred from the machine to a surface that has been lightly dusted with flour. Take a 10-minute break. **(4)** Make a 9-by-12-inch rectangle out of the dough by gently patting it down. Toss together the pecans, cinnamon, brown sugar, and chopped apples in a small bowl. **(5)** Evenly cover the dough with apple mixture. **(6)** Start rolling the dough tightly from the short end. **(7)** In a greased 9x5-inch loaf pan, arrange rolled dough seam-side down. **(8)** After an hour of rising, the dough should have doubled in size, so cover it with a clean dish towel. **(9)** It is recommended to preheat the oven to 175°C. **(10)** To get a beautiful brown crust, bake the bread for 30–35 minutes. **(11)** In a separate dish, combine the powdered sugar with the milk to make the glaze. **(12)** Spread the glaze over the warmed bread. **(13)** After taking the bread out of the pan, let it cool for ten minutes on a wire rack.

RASPBERRY SWIRL BREAD

Total Time: 3 hours 45 minutes | Prep Time: 25 minutes | Yield: 1 loaf

Ingredients:

1 cup warm milk	3 tablespoons butter, softened
3 cups bread flour	1/4 cup sugar
1 1/2 teaspoons salt	2 teaspoons active dry yeast
1/2 cup raspberry jam	1/4 cup powdered sugar
1 tablespoon milk	

Directions:

(1) The bread machine pan should include warm milk, butter, bread flour, sugar, salt, and yeast in the manufacturer's recommended order. **(2)** Select and start the dough cycle. **(3)** Remove the dough from the machine and set it on a lightly floured surface. Let it rest for 10 minutes. **(4)** Roll the dough into a 9x12-inch rectangle. **(5)** Apply raspberry jam equally to the dough. **(6)** Start rolling the dough tightly from a short end. **(7)** In a greased 9x5-inch loaf pan, place the rolled dough seam side down. **(8)** After an hour of rising in a warm spot, or when the dough has multiplied by two, cover with a clean kitchen towel and set aside. **(9)** It is recommended to preheat the oven to 175°C. Put the bread in the oven and bake for 30–35 minutes or until it turns golden brown. *(10)* For the glaze, combine the milk and powdered sugar in a small dish. *(11)* Evenly coat heated bread with glaze. *(12)* Before moving the bread to a wire rack, let it cool for 10 minutes in the pan.

CHOCOLATE MARBLE BREAD

Total Time: 3 hours 30 minutes | Prep Time: 20 minutes | Yield: 1 loaf

Ingredients:

1 cup warm water	3 tablespoons butter, softened
3 cups bread flour	1/4 cup cocoa powder
3 tablespoons sugar	1 1/2 teaspoons salt
2 teaspoons active dry yeast	

Directions:

(1) As advised by the manufacturer, add warm water, butter, bread flour, cocoa powder, sugar, salt, and yeast to the bread machine pan. *(2)* Choose the dough cycle and start. *(3)* Lift half the dough from the machine and set it on a lightly floured board after the dough cycle. Rest for 10 minutes. *(4)* Mix cocoa powder into the remaining dough in the machine until thoroughly blended. *(5)* Roll each piece of dough into a 9x12-inch rectangle. *(6)* Add chocolate dough to normal dough. *(7)* Tightly roll the dough, beginning at the shorter end. *(8)* With the seam side down, transfer the rolled dough to a greased 9x5-inch loaf pan. *(9)* After an hour of being in a warm spot, cover the pan with a clean dish towel and wait for the dough to double in size. *(10)* Set oven temperature to 350°F, or 175°C. *(11)* After 30–35 minutes in the oven, the bread should be golden brown and cooked thoroughly. *(12)* Ten minutes of cooling time in the pan is required before moving the bread to a wire rack.

MAPLE BACON BREAD

Total Time: 3 hours 30 minutes | Prep Time: 15 minutes

Ingredients:

1 cup warm water	2 tablespoons maple syrup
2 tablespoons butter, softened	3 cups bread flour
2 teaspoons active dry yeast	1 teaspoon salt
1/2 cup cooked bacon, crumbled	

Directions:

(1) Melted butter, maple syrup, and warm water should all be combined in the bread machine pan. *(2)* Over the liquid ingredients, add salt, bread flour, and active dry yeast. *(3)* Choose the "Basic" or "White Bread" setting after inserting the bread pan into the bread maker. *(4)* When the machine beeps for add-ins, which is normally around five minutes into the kneading cycle, add the crumbled bacon. *(5)* Shut off the cover and allow the bread maker to finish its cycle. *(6)* When the bread is finished, carefully take it out of the pan and allow it to cool on a wire rack before slicing.

CHEDDAR JALAPENO BREAD

Total Time: 3 hours 45 minutes | Prep Time: 20 minutes

Ingredients:

1 cup warm milk	2 tablespoons olive oil
3 cups bread flour	2 teaspoons active dry yeast
1 teaspoon salt	1 cup shredded cheddar cheese
2 jalapenos, seeded and finely chopped	

Directions:

(1) Transfer the warm milk and olive oil to the bread maker pan. *(2)* Over the liquid ingredients, add salt, bread flour, and active dry yeast. *(3)* Choose the "Basic" or "White Bread" setting after inserting the bread pan into the bread maker. *(4)* About five minutes into the kneading cycle, or when the machine beeps for add-ins, add the chopped jalapenos and shredded cheddar cheese. *(5)* Shut off the cover and allow the bread maker to finish its cycle. *(6)* When the bread is finished, carefully take it out of the pan and allow it to cool on a wire rack before slicing.

HERB AND ONION FOCACCIA

Total Time: 2 hours 30 minutes | Prep Time: 15 minutes | Yield: 1 loaf

Ingredients:

1 cup warm water	2 tablespoons olive oil
3 cups bread flour	1 1/2 teaspoons salt
1 tablespoon sugar	1 tablespoon dried oregano
1 tablespoon dried thyme	1/2 cup chopped onion
2 cloves garlic, minced	2 teaspoons active dry yeast
Additional olive oil for brushing	Coarse sea salt for sprinkling

Directions:

(1) In your Zojirushi bread machine bread pan, add warm water and olive oil. **(2)** Before adding the active dry yeast, salt, sugar, oregano, thyme, chopped onion, minced garlic, and bread flour to the pan, follow the manufacturer's directions. **(3)** Before starting the bread machine, place the pan inside and choose "Dough." Start up the device. **(4)** Take the dough from the bread pan and set it on a lightly floured board. Heat oven to 400°F (200°C). **(5)** A greased baking sheet should hold the rectangle of dough. **(6)** Indent the dough with your fingertips. **(7)** Use olive oil and coarse sea salt to coat the dough. **(8)** Give the dough 30 minutes to rise in a warm place. **(9)** Bake focaccia for 20–25 minutes in a preheated oven until golden brown. **(10)** Remove from oven and cool somewhat before slicing and serving. Enjoy Herb-Onion Focaccia!

CARAMELIZED ONION AND GRUYERE FOCACCIA

Total Time: 2 hours | Prep Time: 30 minutes

Ingredients:

1 large onion, thinly sliced	2 tablespoons olive oil
1 teaspoon sugar	1 teaspoon balsamic vinegar
1 teaspoon salt	1/2 teaspoon black pepper
1 tablespoon fresh thyme leaves	1 cup shredded Gruyere cheese
3 cups bread flour	1 1/2 teaspoons instant yeast
1 teaspoon sugar	1 teaspoon salt
1 1/4 cups warm water	Extra olive oil for greasing and drizzling

Directions:

(1) Pan-heat olive oil on medium. Simmer sliced onions for 20 minutes until caramelized, stirring periodically. **(2)** Stir in sugar, balsamic vinegar, salt, pepper, and thyme. Finish cooking for 5 minutes, then cool. **(3)** Gather the flour, yeast, sugar, and salt in a large basin. Gently incorporate the dough with the heated water. **(4)** After adding flour, knead the dough for 5–7 minutes until it becomes elastic. **(5)** After greasing a basin, transfer the dough and cover it with a dishcloth. Let it rise for at least an hour in a warm place. **(6)** Start the Zojirushi bread machine in "dough" mode. **(7)** After rising, punch down and place the dough in the bread machine. Select "dough" and cycle. **(8)** Grease a baking pan and stretch the dough into a rectangle. Let it rise covered for 30 minutes. **(9)** Preheat oven to 400°F (200°C). **(10)** Cover the dough with caramelized onion mixture and Gruyere. **(11)** Bake 20–25 minutes till bubbly and golden. **(12)** Slice, add olive oil, and serve warm.

MUSHROOM AND THYME FOCACCIA

Total Time: 2 hours 30 minutes | Prep Time: 45 minutes

Ingredients:

1 cup sliced mushrooms	2 tablespoons olive oil
2 cloves garlic, minced	1 tablespoon fresh thyme leaves
1 teaspoon salt	1/2 teaspoon black pepper
3 cups bread flour	1 1/2 teaspoons instant yeast
1 teaspoon sugar	1 teaspoon salt
1 1/4 cups warm water	Extra olive oil for greasing and drizzling

Directions:

(1) Medium-heat olive oil in a skillet. Sauté sliced mushrooms and garlic for 10 minutes until golden brown and soft. Add salt, pepper, and thyme. Remove and cool. **(2)** Gather the flour, yeast, sugar, and salt in a large basin. To make dough, mix warm water with flour and stir. **(3)**

After flouring a surface, knead the dough for about seven to ten minutes or until it becomes elastic. Let the dough rise for one hour in a greased basin covered with a kitchen towel until it has doubled in size. *(4)* Start the Zojirushi bread machine in "dough" mode. *(5)* After rising, punch down and put the dough in the bread machine. Run the "dough" cycle. *(6)* Make a rectangular shape with the dough on a baking sheet that has been buttered. Let it sit covered for half an hour to rise. *(7)* Heat oven to 400°F (200°C). *(8)* Cover the dough with a mushroom mixture. *(9)* Bake 20–25 minutes until golden and bubbling. *(10)* Slice and serve warm with additional olive oil.

FIG AND GOAT CHEESE FOCACCIA

Total Time: 3 hours | Prep Time: 20 minutes

Ingredients:

1 cup warm water	2 1/4 teaspoons active dry yeast
2 1/2 cups all-purpose flour	1 teaspoon salt
2 tablespoons olive oil	1/4 cup fig jam
1/2 cup crumbled goat cheese	2 tablespoons chopped fresh rosemary
Salt and black pepper to taste	

Directions:

(1) Warm water and yeast should be combined in the bread machine pan. Let it sit until foamy, about 5 minutes. *(2)* Toss in the flour, olive oil, and salt. *(3)* Once the dough setting is chosen, turn on the machine. *(4)* When the dough is ready, set the oven temperature to 200°C. *(5)* After the dough is pounded, it is transferred to an oiled baking pan. Draw a rectangle by stretching it out. Evenly cover the dough with fig jam. Top with chopped rosemary and crumbled goat cheese. *(6)* Add black pepper and salt for seasoning. *(7)* Give the focaccia a half-hour to rise. *(8)* To get golden brown edges, bake in a preheated oven for 20–25 minutes. *(9)* Before slicing, remove it from the oven and allow it to cool slightly. Warm servings are recommended.

SPINACH AND FETA FOCACCIA

Total Time: 3 hours | Prep Time: 20 minutes | Serves: 8

Ingredients:

1 cup warm water	2 tablespoons olive oil
3 cups bread flour	1 1/2 teaspoons white sugar
1 1/2 teaspoons salt	2 1/4 teaspoons active dry yeast
1 cup fresh spinach, chopped	1/2 cup crumbled feta cheese
2 tablespoons grated Parmesan cheese	1 teaspoon dried oregano
1 teaspoon garlic powder	Salt and pepper to taste
Extra olive oil for drizzling	

Directions:

(1) As advised by the manufacturer, mix warm water, olive oil, bread flour, sugar, salt, and yeast in the bread machine pan. *(2)* Start the machine with the Dough cycle. *(3)* After the cycle, punch down the dough on a lightly floured surface. Let it rest for 10 minutes. *(4)* Heat the oven to 190°C. Grease or parchment a baking sheet. *(5)* Place the rectangle of dough on the baking sheet. *(6)* Mix spinach, feta, Parmesan, oregano, garlic powder, salt, and pepper in a small bowl. *(7)* Evenly distribute spinach and feta on the dough. *(8)* Make dough dimples using your fingertips. *(9)* Overcoat dough with olive oil. *(10)* The focaccia should be golden brown after 20–25 minutes in the preheated oven. *(11)* After baking, let it cool before slicing. Warm serve.

HAM AND SWISS FOCACCIA

Total Time: 3 hours 15 minutes | Prep Time: 15 minutes | Servings: 8

Ingredients:

1 cup warm water	2 tablespoons olive oil
3 cups bread flour	1 1/2 teaspoons salt
2 teaspoons sugar	2 1/4 teaspoons active dry yeast
1/2 cup diced ham	1/2 cup shredded Swiss cheese

2 tablespoons chopped fresh parsley	1 tablespoon coarse sea salt

Directions:

(1) Warm water and olive oil in the bread machine pan. **(2)** Use the manufacturer's sequence to add bread flour, salt, sugar, and yeast to the pan. **(3)** Choose the dough cycle and start the breadmaker. **(4)** Put the dough on a lightly floured surface after the dough cycle. Be patient for 10 minutes. **(5)** Heat oven to 400°F (200°C). Use parchment or grease a baking pan. **(6)** Turn the dough into a 1/2-inch rectangle on the baking sheet. **(7)** Put diced ham and shredded Swiss cheese on the dough. Chop parsley and add coarse sea salt. **(8)** For 20–25 minutes, bake the focaccia till golden brown and done. **(9)** Before slicing, let the focaccia cool. Warm up and enjoy.

ARTICHOKE AND PARMESAN FOCACCIA

Total Time: 3 hours | Prep Time: 20 minutes

Ingredients:

1 cup warm water	2 tablespoons olive oil
3 cups bread flour	1 1/2 teaspoons salt
2 teaspoons sugar	2 teaspoons active dry yeast
1/2 cup chopped artichoke hearts	1/4 cup grated Parmesan cheese
2 tablespoons chopped fresh rosemary	

Directions:

(1) In the bread machine pan, mix olive oil and warm water. **(2)** In the pan, add bread flour, salt, sugar, and yeast. **(3)** Select the dough cycle and start the machinery. **(4)** Remove the dough from the machine and set it on a lightly floured surface. **(5)** Preheat oven to 400°F (200°C). **(6)** Roll dough into a 1/2-inch rectangle. **(7)** Place dough on a prepared baking sheet. **(8)** Cut artichoke hearts and press them into dough. **(9)** Sprinkle-grated Parmesan and chopped rosemary on dough. **(10)** Let the dough rise for half an hour, covered with a clean dish towel. **(11)** The focaccia should be golden brown after 20–25 minutes in the preheated oven. **(12)** Wait to slice

and serve the focaccia after it cools from the oven.

PEPPERONI AND MOZZARELLA FOCACCIA

Total Time: 3 hours | Prep Time: 20 minutes | Servings: 8

Ingredients:

1 cup warm water	2 tablespoons olive oil
3 cups bread flour	1 1/2 teaspoons salt
1 tablespoon sugar	2 1/4 teaspoons active dry yeast
1/2 cup sliced pepperoni	1 cup shredded mozzarella cheese
1 teaspoon dried oregano	1/2 teaspoon garlic powder
Olive oil for drizzling	

Directions:

(1) As advised by the manufacturer, mix warm water, olive oil, bread flour, salt, sugar, and yeast in the bread machine pan. **(2)** Before turning on the machine, choose the dough cycle. **(3)** Remove the dough from the machine and set it on a lightly floured surface. Punch down and rest the dough for 10 minutes. **(4)** Heat the oven to 200°C. **(5)** Make a rectangle of dough and place it on a prepared baking sheet. **(6)** Put pepperoni and mozzarella cheese in the dough. **(7)** Sprinkle dried oregano and garlic powder over top. **(8)** Spread olive oil on flatbread. **(9)** Let the focaccia rise for 30 minutes under loose plastic wrap. **(10)** Preheat oven and bake for 20–25 minutes till golden brown. **(11)** Cool the focaccia before slicing and serving.

SUN-DRIED TOMATO AND OLIVE FOCACCIA

Total Time: 3 hours 30 minutes | Prep Time: 15 minutes | Yield: 1 loaf

Ingredients:

1 cup warm water (110°F)	2 1/4 teaspoons active dry yeast
2 1/2 cups all-purpose flour	2 tablespoons olive oil
1 teaspoon salt	1/4 cup chopped sun-dried tomatoes

| 1/4 cup chopped black olives | 2 tablespoons chopped fresh basil |
| Coarse sea salt for sprinkling | |

Directions:

(1) In the bread machine pan, mix yeast and warm water. Wait 5 minutes for frothing. *(2)* Season the pan with salt, olive oil, and flour. *(3)* Select the dough cycle and begin. *(4)* Remove the dough from the dough cycle and place it in a basin that has been lightly greased. To let it double in size, cover it in a clean kitchen towel after an hour of raising it in a warm spot. *(5)* Heat the oven to 200°C. Punch down the dough and place it on a prepared baking sheet. Stretch the dough to fit the pan gently. *(6)* Evenly press sun-dried tomatoes, olives, and basil into dough. Add olive oil and coarse sea salt. *(7)* Bake till golden brown, 20–25 minutes. Cool gently before slicing and serving.

CARAMELIZED ONION AND ROSEMARY FOCACCIA

Total Time: 3 hours 45 minutes | Prep Time: 30 minutes | Yield: 1 loaf

Ingredients:

1 cup warm water (110°F)	2 1/4 teaspoons active dry yeast
2 1/2 cups all-purpose flour	2 tablespoons olive oil
1 teaspoon salt	2 large onions, thinly sliced
2 tablespoons butter	2 tablespoons chopped fresh rosemary
Coarse sea salt for sprinkling	

Directions:

(1) Add yeast and warm water to the bread machine pan. Allow to foam for 5 minutes. *(2)* Salt, flour, and olive oil in the pan. *(3)* Start the dough cycle. *(4)* Butter should be melted in a pan set over medium heat as the dough is being kneaded. For 20 to 25 minutes, as the cut onions caramelize, stir them occasionally. Set aside to cool. *(5)* Afterward, oil a basin and transfer the dough to it. Simply place it in a warm spot for an hour, cover it with a clean kitchen towel, and it

will double in size. *(6)* The recommended oven temperature is 400 degrees Fahrenheit (200 degrees Celsius). *(7)* After the dough has been pounded, it should be transferred to a baking sheet. Carefully pull the dough taut until it fits into the pan. *(8)* Spread dough with caramelized onions. Sprinkle coarse sea salt and chopped rosemary. *(9)* Bake till golden, 20–25 minutes. Slice and serve after cooling.

GARLIC AND HERB FOCACCIA

Total Time: 3 hours 30 minutes | Prep Time: 15 minutes

Ingredients:

1 cup warm water	2 1/4 teaspoons active dry yeast
2 1/2 cups bread flour	two tablespoons of olive oil
1 teaspoon salt	2 cloves garlic, minced
1 tablespoon fresh rosemary, chopped	1 tablespoon fresh thyme leaves
Coarse sea salt for sprinkling	

Directions:

(1) In the bread machine pan, mix yeast and warm water. Let sit for 5 minutes to foam. *(2)* To the yeast mixture, add bread flour, olive oil, and salt. *(3)* Start your bread maker on dough mode. *(4)* When the dough is done, preheat the oven to 400°F (200°C). Grease or parchment a baking sheet. *(5)* Punch down the dough and place it on the baking sheet. Press the dough evenly into the pan. *(6)* Dress the dough with olive oil. Evenly sprinkle minced garlic, rosemary, thyme, and coarse sea salt. *(7)* Thirty minutes beneath a clean kitchen towel in a warm place will let the dough rise. *(8)* A golden brown color may be achieved by placing it in a preheated oven for twenty to twenty-five minutes. *(9)* Slicing focaccia requires some cooling. Serve hot and enjoy!

SESAME SEED FOCACCIA

Total Time: 3 hours 30 minutes | Prep Time: 15 minutes | Yield: 1 loaf

Ingredients:

1 cup warm water	2 1/4 teaspoons active dry yeast
2 1/2 cups bread flour	1 teaspoon salt
2 tablespoons olive oil	2 tablespoons sesame seeds
Additional olive oil for greasing and drizzling	Coarse sea salt for sprinkling

Directions:

(1) In the bread machine pan, mix yeast and warm water. Let sit 5-10 minutes to foam. *(2)* Put bread flour, salt, and olive oil in the pan. *(3)* Pick the dough setting and put the bread machine pan in. Start the machine. *(4)* Remove the dough from the machine and set it on a lightly floured surface. *(5)* Heat the oven to 200°C. Grease a baking sheet with olive oil. *(6)* Transfer the dough to the baking sheet after stretching and shaping it into a 1/2-inch rectangle or circle. *(7)* Press your hands into the dough to create depressions. Pour olive oil over the dough and sprinkle sesame seeds and coarse sea salt. *(8)* Let the dough rise in a warm place for 30–45 minutes under a clean kitchen towel. *(9)* Preheat oven and bake for 20–25 minutes till golden brown. *(10)* After baking, let it cool before slicing and serving.

PESTO AND PINE NUT FOCACCIA

Total Time: 4 hours | Prep Time: 20 minutes | Yield: 1 loaf

Ingredients:

1 cup warm water	2 1/4 teaspoons active dry yeast
2 1/2 cups bread flour	1 teaspoon salt
2 tablespoons olive oil	1/4 cup prepared pesto sauce
1/4 cup pine nuts	Additional olive oil for greasing

Directions:

(1) In the bread machine pan, mix yeast and warm water. Let sit 5-10 minutes to foam. *(2)* Put bread flour, salt, and olive oil in the pan. *(3)* Pick the dough setting and put the bread machine pan in. Start the machine. *(4)* Remove the dough from the machine and set it on a lightly floured surface. *(5)* Heat the oven to 200°C. Grease a baking sheet with olive oil. *(6)* Transfer the dough to the baking sheet after stretching and shaping it into a 1/2-inch rectangle or circle. *(7)* Apply pesto sauce evenly to the dough. *(8)* Sprinkle pine nuts over pesto. *(9)* Let the dough rise in a warm place for 30–45 minutes under a clean kitchen towel. *(10)* Preheat oven and bake for 20–25 minutes till golden brown. *(11)* After baking, let it cool before slicing and serving.

LEMON AND HERB FOCACCIA

Total Time: 3 hours | Prep Time: 15 minutes

Ingredients:

1 cup warm water	2 tablespoons olive oil
3 cups bread flour	1 1/2 teaspoons salt
1 tablespoon sugar	Zest of 1 lemon
2 tablespoons fresh rosemary, chopped	1 tablespoon fresh thyme leaves
Extra olive oil for drizzling	Coarse sea salt for sprinkling

Directions:

(1) In the bread machine's pan, combine the olive oil and hot water. Season with salt, sugar, rosemary, thyme, lemon zest, and bread flour. *(2)* Start the bread machine's dough cycle after placing the pan inside. *(3)* Preheating the oven to 200°C is the next step after the dough is ready. *(4)* After stretching the dough to fit, transfer it to a baking sheet that has been oiled. *(5)* Allow it to rise for half an hour, covered with a damp kitchen towel. *(6)* Poke holes in the dough using your fingers once it has risen. *(7)* Toss with some coarse sea salt and olive oil. *(8)* If you want a golden brown finish, bake it for 20 to 25 minutes in a preheated oven. *(9)* Wait for it to cool a bit before cutting and serving.

PARMESAN AND BLACK PEPPER FOCACCIA

Total Time: 3 hours 30 minutes | Prep Time: 15 minutes

Ingredients:

1 cup lukewarm water	2 tablespoons olive oil
3 cups bread flour	2 teaspoons sugar
1 1/2 teaspoons salt	1 tablespoon instant yeast

1/4 cup grated Parmesan cheese	1 teaspoon freshly ground black pepper
Additional olive oil for brushing	Coarse sea salt for sprinkling

Directions:

(1) In the sequence indicated by the manufacturer, add water, olive oil, bread flour, sugar, salt, and yeast to the bread machine pan. *(2)* Start your bread maker on dough mode. *(3)* After the dough cycle, remove it from the machine and place it on a lightly floured board. For a greased baking sheet, punch down and shape the dough into a rectangle. *(4)* Rest the dough for 30 minutes in a clean kitchen towel. *(5)* Heat the oven to 200°C. *(6)* Make indentations in the dough with your fingertips. *(7)* Rub olive oil into the dough, then sprinkle grated Parmesan and crushed black pepper on top. *(8)* A golden brown crust can be achieved by preheating the oven for twenty to twenty-five minutes. Once baked, garnish with coarse sea salt and drizzle with olive oil. *(9)* Cool gently before slicing and serving.

SUNDRIED TOMATO AND MOZZARELLA FOCACCIA

Total Time: 2 hours 30 minutes | Prep Time: 15 minutes | Servings: 8

Ingredients:

1 cup warm water	2 1/4 teaspoons active dry yeast
2 1/2 cups all-purpose flour	2 tablespoons olive oil
1 teaspoon salt	1/4 cup chopped sundried tomatoes (drained if packed in oil)
1/2 cup shredded mozzarella cheese	1 tablespoon chopped fresh rosemary (optional)
Additional olive oil for drizzling	Coarse sea salt for sprinkling

Directions:

(1) In the bread machine pan, mix yeast and warm water. Wait 5 minutes for foam. *(2)* Season the pan with salt, olive oil, and flour. Begin by selecting the dough setting on the machine. *(3)* Move the dough to a gently floured surface after the dough cycle is complete. After the dough has been kneaded, form it into a ball. *(4)* Set the oven to a high temperature (200°C). Melt some parchment paper or foil and coat a baking sheet. *(5)* Apply the dough to the baking sheet by rolling it into a 1/2-inch rectangle. *(6)* Press fingers into the dough to make dimples. Sprinkle chopped sundried tomatoes, shredded mozzarella, and fresh rosemary on the dough and drizzle with olive oil. Gently press toppings into the dough. *(7)* For at least half an hour, make sure the dough is in a warm, draft-free place to rise. *(8)* The focaccia should be golden brown and cooked through after 20–25 minutes in the preheated oven. *(9)* Sprinkle coarse sea salt immediately after baking. Cool gently before slicing and serving. Enjoy your Sundried Tomato and Mozzarella Focaccia!

HONEY AND WALNUT FOCACCIA

Total Time: 3 hours | Prep Time: 20 minutes

Ingredients:

1 cup warm water	2 1/4 teaspoons active dry yeast
2 1/2 cups all-purpose flour	2 tablespoons honey
1 teaspoon salt	3 tablespoons olive oil
1/2 cup chopped walnuts	Extra olive oil for drizzling

Directions:

(1) In the bread machine pan, mix yeast and warm water. Wait 5 minutes for foam. *(2)* Put flour, honey, salt, and olive oil in the pan. *(3)* Set your bread machine to "Dough" or "Manual" and start. *(4)* Place the dough on a lightly floured board and equally distribute the chopped walnuts. *(5)* Heat the oven to 200°C. *(6)* Stretch dough to fit an olive oil-greased baking pan. *(7)* Let the dough rise for 30 minutes under a clean kitchen towel. *(8)* After rising, finger-dimple the dough and add olive oil. *(9)* Bake till golden brown, 20–25 minutes. *(10)* Cool gently before slicing and serving.

BLUE CHEESE AND WALNUT FOCACCIA

Total Time: 3 hours 15 minutes | Prep Time: 25 minutes

Ingredients:

1 cup warm water	2 1/4 teaspoons active dry yeast
2 1/2 cups all-purpose flour	1 tablespoon honey
1 teaspoon salt	3 tablespoons olive oil
1/2 cup crumbled blue cheese	1/2 cup chopped walnuts
Extra olive oil for drizzling	

Directions:

(1) In the bread machine pan, mix yeast and warm water. Wait 5 minutes for foam. **(2)** Put flour, honey, salt, and olive oil in the pan. **(3)** Set your bread machine to "Dough" or "Manual" and start. **(4)** After flouring a surface, transfer the dough and, until evenly distributed, stir in the crumbled blue cheese and chopped walnuts. **(5)** Heat the oven to 200°C. **(6)** Stretch dough to fit an olive oil-greased baking pan. **(7)** Let the dough rise for 30 minutes under a clean kitchen towel. **(8)** After rising, finger-dimple the dough and add olive oil. **(9)** Bake till golden brown, 25-30 minutes. **(10)** Cool gently before slicing and serving.

GARLIC AND PARMESAN BREADSTICKS

Total Time: 2 hours | Prep Time: 15 minutes | Makes: 12 breadsticks

Ingredients:

1 cup warm water	2 1/4 teaspoons active dry yeast
2 tablespoons olive oil	1 tablespoon sugar
3 cups bread flour	1 teaspoon salt
2 cloves garlic, minced	1/4 cup grated Parmesan cheese
2 tablespoons chopped fresh parsley	2 tablespoons melted butter

Directions:

(1) In the bread machine pan, mix warm water, yeast, olive oil, and sugar. Wait 5 minutes for the yeast to froth. **(2)** Season pan with bread flour and salt. Select and start the dough cycle. **(3)** After the dough cycle, place it on a lightly floured surface. Roll each piece into an 8-inch rope in 12 equal segments. **(4)** Heat the oven to 190°C. Parchment a baking sheet. **(5)** Place breadsticks on the baking sheet with space between them. Allow to rise for 30 minutes under a clean kitchen towel. **(6)** Mix minced garlic, grated Parmesan, and chopped fresh parsley in a small basin. **(7)** Spread melted butter on rising breadsticks and sprinkle garlic-Parmesan mixture on top. **(8)** Bake, covered, for 15–20 minutes on high heat or until brown. Enjoy while hot!

HERB AND CHEESE BREADSTICKS

Total Time: 2 hours 30 minutes | Prep Time: 15 minutes | Yield: 12 breadsticks

Ingredients:

1 cup warm water	2 tablespoons olive oil
3 cups bread flour	2 tablespoons granulated sugar
1 teaspoon salt	1 tablespoon dried Italian herbs (basil, oregano, thyme)
1 teaspoon garlic powder	1 teaspoon onion powder
1 tablespoon active dry yeast	1 cup shredded mozzarella cheese
1/4 cup grated Parmesan cheese	1/4 cup melted butter
Additional grated Parmesan cheese for topping	Additional dried herbs for topping

Directions:

(1) Fill the bread machine pan with warm water and olive oil. **(2)** In a separate bowl, mix bread flour, sugar, salt, dried Italian herbs, garlic powder, onion powder, and active dry yeast. **(3)** Over the water and oil, add the dry ingredients to the bread machine pan. **(4)** Press start on the bread machine's "Dough" cycle. **(5)** Place the dough on a floured board after the bread machine cycle. Preheat oven to 375°F (190°C). **(6)** Roll each dough slice into a long rope. **(7)** Place ropes on a prepared baking sheet with room between breadsticks. **(8)** Sprinkle shredded mozzarella and Parmesan cheese on the breadsticks after melting the butter. **(9)** Let breadsticks rise 20–30 minutes. **(10)** Brown and finish cooking in a preheated oven, stirring once or twice. This should take around 15 to 20 minutes. **(11)** Brush with more melted butter after baking. If preferred, add grated Parmesan and dried herbs. *(12)* Serve hot and relish!

SESAME SEED BREADSTICKS

Total Time: 3 hours | Prep Time: 15 minutes

Ingredients:

1 cup warm water	2 tablespoons olive oil
3 cups bread flour	2 teaspoons sugar
1 ½ teaspoons salt	2 ¼ teaspoons active dry yeast
¼ cup sesame seeds	1 egg, beaten (for egg wash)
Coarse sea salt for sprinkling	

Directions:

(1) Following the manufacturer's recommendations, put warm water, olive oil, bread flour, sugar, salt, and yeast in the pan of the bread machine. *(2)* Choose the Dough cycle and hit the Start button. *(3)* After the dough cycle is finished, turn the oven up to 375°F, or 190°C. *(4)* Roll each of the 12 equal portions of dough into a 10-inch rope. *(5)* Leaving room between each rope, place the ropes on a baking sheet coated with paper. *(6)* Each rope should be brushed with a beaten egg and then dusted with coarse sea salt and sesame seeds. *(7)* Roast for 15 to 20 minutes or until browned on top. *(8)* After removing it from the oven, set it on a wire rack to cool for serving. These breadsticks, topped with sesame seeds, are delicious.

BACON AND CHEDDAR BREADSTICKS

Total Time: 3 hours 15 minutes | Prep Time: 20 minutes

Ingredients:

1 cup warm milk	2 tablespoons butter, melted
3 cups bread flour	2 teaspoons sugar
1 ½ teaspoons salt	2 ¼ teaspoons active dry yeast
6 slices bacon, cooked and crumbled	1 cup shredded cheddar cheese
1 egg, beaten (for egg wash)	

Directions:

(1) Following the manufacturer's recommendations, add warm milk, melted butter, bread flour, sugar, salt, and yeast to the bread machine pan. *(2)* Choose the Dough cycle and hit the Start button. *(3)* After the dough cycle is finished, turn the oven up to 375°F, or 190°C. *(4)* Make a rectangle out of the dough, spreading it out so it's 1/4 inch thick. *(5)* Shredded cheddar cheese and crumbled bacon should be distributed evenly over the dough. *(6)* Form a log form by carefully rolling the dough, beginning with one long side. *(7)* After slicing the log into twelve equal pieces, place them on a parchment-lined baking sheet. *(8)* Beat an egg and brush it across each slice. *(9)* Melt the cheese and brown the crust in the oven for 20 to 25 minutes. *(10)* Take it out of the oven and allow it to cool down a little before serving. These breadsticks with bacon and cheddar cheese are guaranteed to be popular!

ROSEMARY AND SEA SALT BREADSTICKS

Total Time: 3 hours 30 minutes | Prep Time: 25 minutes

Ingredients:

1 cup warm water	2 tablespoons olive oil
3 cups bread flour	2 teaspoons sugar
1 ½ teaspoons salt	2 ¼ teaspoons active dry yeast
2 tablespoons fresh rosemary, chopped	Coarse sea salt for sprinkling

Directions:

(1) Following the manufacturer's recommendations, put warm water, olive oil, bread flour, sugar, salt, and yeast in the pan of the bread machine. *(2)* Choose the Dough cycle and hit the Start button. *(3)* After the dough cycle is finished, turn the oven up to 375°F, or 190°C. *(4)* Make a rectangle out of the dough, spreading it out so it's 1/4 inch thick. *(5)* Scatter the chopped rosemary evenly over the dough. *(6)* Slice the dough into 12 equal pieces using a pizza cutter or a sharp knife. After twisting each strip, place them on a parchment-lined baking sheet. *(7)* Put in a pinch or two of coarse sea salt. *(8)* Roast for 15 to 20 minutes or until browned on

top. *(9)* Take it out of the oven and allow it to cool down a little before serving. These breadsticks with sea salt and rosemary are a great side dish for any meal!

SUN-DRIED TOMATO AND OLIVE BREADSTICKS

Total Time: 3 hours 30 minutes | Prep Time: 15 minutes | Yield: 12 breadsticks

Ingredients:

1 cup warm water	2 tablespoons olive oil
3 cups bread flour	1 teaspoon salt
2 teaspoons sugar	1 1/2 teaspoons active dry yeast
1/3 cup chopped sun-dried tomatoes	1/4 cup chopped black olives
Cornmeal, for dusting	

Directions:

(1) Olive oil and warm water should be combined in the bread machine pan. *(2)* As directed by the maker, add the bread flour, sugar, salt, and yeast to the pan. *(3)* Choose the Dough cycle and hit the Start button. *(4)* After the dough cycle is finished, move the dough to a surface that has been lightly dusted and work in the black olives and sun-dried tomatoes until they are uniformly distributed. *(5)* Roll out the dough into 12 equal sections, then shape each into a breadstick. *(6)* After dusting a baking sheet with cornmeal, set the breadsticks on it, cover it with a fresh kitchen towel, and leave it in a warm area for half an hour. *(7)* Turn the oven on to 190°C. *(8)* Bake the breadsticks until golden brown, 15 to 20 minutes. *(9)* Enjoy and warm up!

CINNAMON SUGAR BREADSTICKS

Total Time: 3 hours 15 minutes | Prep Time: 10 minutes | Yield: 12 breadsticks

Ingredients:

1 cup warm milk	3 tablespoons butter, melted
3 cups bread flour	1/4 cup granulated sugar
1 teaspoon salt	2 teaspoons ground cinnamon
1 1/2 teaspoons active dry yeast	1/4 cup granulated sugar (for coating)
1 teaspoon ground cinnamon (for coating)	

Directions:

(1) Melted butter and warm milk should be combined in the bread machine pan. *(2)* In the sequence suggested by the manufacturer, add yeast, sugar, salt, cinnamon, and bread flour to the pan. *(3)* Choose the Dough cycle and hit the Start button. *(4)* After the dough cycle finishes, remove the dough from the machine and place it on a floured board. Divide the dough into 12 equal sections. *(5)* Roll each piece into a stick, similar to a breadstick. *(6)* A quarter cup of granulated sugar and one teaspoon of cinnamon should be mixed together in a small basin. *(7)* To get a uniform coating, roll each breadstick in the cinnamon sugar mixture. *(8)* Arrange the coated breadsticks onto a parchment paper-lined baking sheet. *(9)* Place in a warm location for half an hour after covering with a fresh kitchen towel. *(10)* Turn the oven on to 190°C. *(11)* For 12 to 15 minutes, or until they are gently golden, bake the breadsticks. *(12)* Enjoy and warm up!

PARMESAN AND BLACK PEPPER BREADSTICKS

Total Time: 3 hours 30 minutes | Prep Time: 15 minutes | Yield: 12 breadsticks

Ingredients:

1 cup warm water	2 tablespoons olive oil
3 cups bread flour	1 teaspoon salt
2 teaspoons sugar	1 1/2 teaspoons active dry yeast
1/4 cup grated Parmesan cheese	1 teaspoon freshly ground black pepper
2 tablespoons melted butter	2 tablespoons grated Parmesan cheese (for topping)

Directions:

(1) Olive oil and warm water should be combined in the bread machine pan. *(2)* As directed by the maker, add the bread flour, sugar, salt, and yeast to the pan. *(3)* Choose the Dough cycle and hit the Start button. *(4)* Upon completion of the dough

cycle, transfer the dough to a lightly dusted surface and, using your fingertips, incorporate 1/4 cup of grated Parmesan cheese and black pepper until the ingredients are well distributed. **(5)** Roll out the dough into 12 equal sections, then shape each into a breadstick. **(6)** Arrange the breadsticks on a parchment paper-lined baking sheet. **(7)** Place in a warm location for half an hour after covering with a fresh kitchen towel. **(8)** Turn the oven on to 190°C. **(9)** Melt butter and then add two teaspoons of grated Parmesan cheese to the rising breadsticks. **(10)** Roast for 15 to 20 minutes or until browned on top. **(11)** Enjoy and warm up!

GARLIC KNOTS WITH PARMESAN

Total Time: 3 hours 45 minutes | Prep Time: 20 minutes | Yield: 12 knots

Ingredients:

1 cup warm milk	3 tablespoons olive oil
3 cups bread flour	1 teaspoon salt
2 teaspoons sugar	1 1/2 teaspoons active dry yeast
3 cloves garlic, minced	2 tablespoons chopped fresh parsley
1/4 cup grated Parmesan cheese	2 tablespoons melted butter
2 tablespoons grated Parmesan cheese (for topping)	

Directions:

(1) Warm milk and olive oil should be combined in the bread machine pan. **(2)** As directed by the maker, add the bread flour, sugar, salt, and yeast to the pan. **(3)** Choose the Dough cycle and hit the Start button. **(4)** Upon completion of the dough cycle, transfer the dough to a floured board and, using your fingers, rub in the Parmesan cheese, chopped parsley, and minced garlic until everything is evenly distributed. **(5)** Make 12 equal pieces of dough by rolling it out, and then roll out each piece into a rope. **(6)** Place each rope on a baking sheet covered with parchment paper and tie it into a knot. **(7)** Place in a warm location for half an hour after covering with a fresh kitchen towel. **(8)** Turn the oven on to 190°C. **(9)**

Melt butter and sprinkle grated Parmesan cheese over the rising knots. **(10)** Roast for 18 to 22 minutes or until browned. **(11)** Enjoy and warm up!

CHEDDAR JALAPENO BREADSTICKS

Total Time: 3 hours 30 minutes | Prep Time: 15 minutes | Yield: 12 breadsticks

Ingredients:

1 cup warm water	2 tablespoons olive oil
3 cups bread flour	1 teaspoon salt
2 teaspoons sugar	1 1/2 teaspoons active dry yeast
1 cup shredded sharp cheddar cheese	2 jalapeno peppers, seeded and finely chopped
Cornmeal, for dusting	

Directions:

(1) Olive oil and warm water should be combined in the bread machine pan. **(2)** As directed by the maker, add the bread flour, sugar, salt, and yeast to the pan. **(3)** Choose the Dough cycle and hit the Start button. **(4)** Turn the dough out onto a floured surface and mix in the chopped jalapeño peppers and shredded cheddar cheese until well incorporated once the dough cycle is done. **(5)** Roll out the dough into 12 equal sections, then shape each into a breadstick. **(6)** After dusting a baking sheet with cornmeal, set the breadsticks on it, cover it with a fresh kitchen towel, and leave it in a warm area for half an hour. **(7)** Turn the oven on to 190°C. **(8)** Bake the breadsticks until golden brown, 15 to 20 minutes. **(9)** Enjoy and warm up!

SPINACH AND FETA BREADSTICKS

Total Time: 3 hours | Prep Time: 20 minutes | Yield: 12 breadsticks

Ingredients:

1 cup packed fresh spinach leaves, chopped	1/2 cup crumbled feta cheese
3 cups bread flour	1 1/4 teaspoons active dry yeast
1 teaspoon salt	1 tablespoon granulated sugar
1 cup warm water	2 tablespoons olive oil

1 tablespoon dried oregano

1 tablespoon garlic powder

1 tablespoon sesame seeds (optional)

Directions:

(1) Following the manufacturer's directions, add warm water, olive oil, salt, sugar, bread flour, and yeast to the bread machine pan. (2) Turn on the dough cycle and begin operating the machine. (3) After the dough cycle is finished, take the dough and lay it out on a surface dusted with flour. (4) Set oven temperature to 190°C. (5) Flatten the dough into a rectangle that is approximately 1/4 inch thick. Chop spinach, feta cheese crumbles, dried oregano, and garlic powder should be evenly distributed over the dough. (6) Form the dough into a log by rolling it tightly along one long edge. (7) Make 12 equal cuts in the log. (8) Arrange the pieces on a parchment-lined baking sheet, being sure to leave some space between each. (9) Sprinkle with sesame seeds if you like. (10) Cook for 15 to 20 minutes or until a golden brown color develops. (11) Graze while it's still warm!

EVERYTHING BAGEL BREADSTICKS

Total Time: 3 hours 15 minutes | Prep Time: 25 minutes | Yield: 12 breadsticks

Ingredients:

3 cups bread flour	1 1/4 teaspoons active dry yeast
1 teaspoon salt	1 tablespoon granulated sugar
1 cup warm water	2 tablespoons olive oil
2 tablespoons everything bagel seasoning	

Directions:

(1) Follow the manufacturer's directions for the bread machine pan to mix the following Ingredients: warm water, olive oil, salt, sugar, bread flour, and yeast. (2) Turn on the dough cycle and press the start button. (3) Take the dough out of the machine and set it on a floured surface after the dough cycle is finished. (4) Turn the oven on high heat (375°F, 190°C). (5) Cut the dough into a rectangle with a thickness of approximately 1/4 inch. (6) Make sure to properly distribute the bagel spice over the dough. (7) Make 12 equal pieces of dough. (8) With enough room between each piece, arrange the pieces on a parchment-lined baking sheet. (9) Brown the top by baking it for around fifteen to twenty minutes. (10) Graze when hot and savor!

HONEY MUSTARD AND PRETZEL BREADSTICKS

Total Time: 3 hours 30 minutes | Prep Time: 30 minutes | Yield: 12 breadsticks

Ingredients:

3 cups bread flour	1 1/4 teaspoons active dry yeast
1 teaspoon salt	1 tablespoon granulated sugar
1 cup warm water	2 tablespoons olive oil
1/4 cup honey mustard	1/2 cup crushed pretzels

Directions:

(1) Follow the manufacturer's directions for the bread machine pan to mix the following Ingredients: warm water, olive oil, salt, sugar, bread flour, and yeast. (2) Turn on the dough cycle and press the start button. (3) Take the dough out of the machine and set it on a floured surface after the dough cycle is finished. (4) Turn the oven on high heat (375°F, 190°C). (5) Cut the dough into a rectangle with a thickness of approximately 1/4 inch. (6) Evenly distribute the honey mustard over the dough. (7) Top the honey mustard with crushed pretzels. (8) Make 12 equal pieces of dough. (9) With enough room between each piece, arrange the pieces on a parchment-lined baking sheet. (10) Brown the top by baking it for around fifteen to twenty minutes. (11) Graze when hot and savor!

MAPLE BACON BREADSTICKS

Total Time: 3 hours 30 minutes | Prep Time: 20 minutes

Ingredients:

1 cup warm water	2 tablespoons maple syrup
1 tablespoon olive oil	3 cups bread flour
1 teaspoon salt	2 teaspoons active dry yeast

6 slices cooked bacon, crumbled	1/4 cup grated Parmesan cheese
2 tablespoons chopped fresh parsley	

Directions:

(1) The bread machine pan should include warm water, maple syrup, and olive oil. *(2)* In sequence, as advised by the manufacturer, add bread flour, salt, and yeast to the pan. *(3)* Switch to the dough and start the machine. *(4)* Take the dough out of the machine and split it into twelve equal pieces. *(5)* Roll each portion into a 10-inch thin rope. *(6)* Place the ropes spaced apart on a parchment-lined baking sheet. *(7)* Let breadsticks rise in a warm location for 30 minutes under a clean kitchen towel. *(8)* Preheat oven to 375°F (190°C). *(9)* Scatter crumbled bacon, Parmesan cheese, and chopped parsley over the breadsticks. *(10)* Bake until golden brown and cooked through 15-18 minutes. *(11)* After baking, let cool before serving. Take some Maple Bacon Breadsticks!

FIG AND GOAT CHEESE BREADSTICKS

Total Time: 3 hours 30 minutes | Prep Time: 20 minutes

Ingredients:

1 cup warm water	2 tablespoons honey
1 tablespoon olive oil	3 cups bread flour
1 teaspoon salt	2 teaspoons active dry yeast
1/2 cup chopped dried figs	4 ounces goat cheese, crumbled
1/4 cup chopped walnuts	2 tablespoons honey for drizzling

Directions:

(1) The bread machine pan should include warm water, honey, and olive oil. *(2)* In sequence, as advised by the manufacturer, add bread flour, salt, and yeast to the pan. *(3)* Switch to the dough and start the machine. *(4)* Take the dough out of the machine and split it into twelve equal pieces. *(5)* Roll each portion into a 10-inch thin rope. *(6)* Place the ropes spaced apart on a parchment-lined baking sheet. *(7)* Let breadsticks rise in a warm location for 30 minutes under a clean kitchen towel. *(8)* Preheat oven to 375°F (190°C). *(9)* Sprinkle chopped dried figs, crumbled goat cheese, and chopped walnuts evenly over the breadsticks. *(10)* Bake until golden brown and cooked through 15-18 minutes. *(11)* Serve honey-drizzled after baking. Fig and goat cheese breadsticks, enjoy!

CARAMELIZED ONION AND GRUYERE BREADSTICKS

Total Time: 3 hours | Prep Time: 20 minutes | Servings: 12 breadsticks

Ingredients:

1 cup warm water	2 tablespoons olive oil
3 cups bread flour	2 teaspoons sugar
1 teaspoon salt	1 teaspoon active dry yeast
1 large onion, thinly sliced	1 tablespoon butter
1 cup grated Gruyere cheese	2 tablespoons chopped fresh thyme

Directions:

(1) Olive oil and warm water in the bread machine pan. *(2)* Pan-add bread flour, sugar, salt, and yeast. *(3)* Start the bread machine in Dough mode. *(4)* Cook onions while kneading bread. Add onions and butter to a pan over medium-low heat. 20–25 minutes, stirring periodically, until onions are caramelized and golden brown. Chill. *(5)* Once the dough cycle is complete, punch it down on a lightly floured surface. Do nothing for 10 minutes. *(6)* Make a 12x16-inch dough rectangle. *(7)* Spread caramelized onions on dough, then grated Gruyere and chopped thyme. *(8)* Beginning on one long edge, begin to roll the dough into a log shape. Use a sharp knife to cut the log into 12 equal pieces. *(9)* Place the pieces spaced apart on a parchment-lined baking sheet. *(10)* In a warm location, cover with a clean kitchen towel and let rise till doubled for 30–45 minutes. *(11)* Prepare the oven at 375°F (190°C). *(12)* Bake breadsticks 15-20 minutes till golden (golden brown). *(13)* Enjoy warm!

LEMON AND HERB BREADSTICKS

Total Time: 3 hours 30 minutes | Prep Time: 15 minutes | Yield: 12 breadsticks

Ingredients:

1 cup warm water	2 tablespoons olive oil

3 cups bread flour	1 tablespoon sugar
1 teaspoon salt	Zest of 1 lemon
1 tablespoon dried mixed herbs (such as thyme, rosemary, and oregano)	2 1/4 teaspoons active dry yeast
2 tablespoons melted butter	Sea salt for sprinkling

Directions:

(1) Warm water, olive oil, bread flour, sugar, salt, lemon zest, herbs, and yeast should all be combined in the bread machine pan according to the manufacturer's recommendations. **(2)** Press start after selecting the dough cycle. **(3)** After the dough cycle is finished, take the dough out of the machine and split it into 12 equal pieces. Make a 10-inch rope out of each section. **(4)** Spread some oil on a baking sheet, arrange the ropes on top, cover with a clean dish cloth, and let aside to rise for 30 minutes in a warm place. **(5)** Set oven temperature to 190°C. **(6)** Sprinkle sea salt on top of the rising breadsticks after brushing them with melted butter. **(7)** Brown in the oven for 15 to 18 minutes or until golden. Enjoy while warm!

BLUE CHEESE AND WALNUT BREADSTICKS

Total Time: 3 hours 45 minutes | Prep Time: 20 minutes | Yield: 12 breadsticks

Ingredients:

1 cup warm milk	2 tablespoons olive oil
3 cups bread flour	2 tablespoons granulated sugar
1 teaspoon salt	1/2 cup crumbled blue cheese
1/2 cup chopped walnuts	2 1/4 teaspoons active dry yeast
2 tablespoons melted butter	Freshly ground black pepper for sprinkling

Directions:

(1) Following the manufacturer's recommendations, add warm milk, olive oil, bread flour, sugar, salt, blue cheese, walnuts, and yeast to the bread machine pan. **(2)** Choose the dough cycle and hit the start button. **(3)** Take the dough out of the machine and split it into 12 equal chunks after the dough cycle is finished.

Each part should roll into a 10-inch rope. **(4)** After brushing the baking sheet with oil, spread the ropes out and cover them with a clean dishcloth. Set away to rise for 30 minutes in a warm spot. **(5)** Turn the oven on to 190°C. **(6)** Melt butter and sprinkle freshly ground black pepper on the rising breadsticks. **(7)** Fry for 15 to 18 minutes or until well-browned. **(8)** Enjoy and warm up!

GARLIC PARMESAN TWISTS

Total Time: 3 hours 30 minutes | Prep Time: 15 minutes | Yield: 12 breadsticks

Ingredients:

1 cup warm water	2 tablespoons olive oil
3 cups bread flour	1 tablespoon granulated sugar
1 teaspoon salt	3 cloves garlic, minced
1/4 cup grated Parmesan cheese	2 1/4 teaspoons active dry yeast
2 tablespoons melted butter	1 tablespoon chopped fresh parsley

Directions:

(1) Following the manufacturer's instructions, put the warm water, olive oil, bread flour, sugar, salt, minced garlic, Parmesan cheese, and yeast in the bread machine pan. **(2)** Choose the dough cycle and hit the start button. **(3)** Take the dough out of the machine and split it into 12 equal chunks after the dough cycle is finished. Each part should roll into a 10-inch rope. **(4)** Place each rope on a baking sheet that has been oiled and twist it. Place in a warm location for half an hour after covering with a fresh kitchen towel. **(5)** Turn the oven on to 190°C. **(6)** After applying melted butter to the risen breadsticks, top with freshly chopped parsley. **(7)** Fry for 15 to 18 minutes or until well-browned. **(8)** Enjoy and warm up!

CHOCOLATE HAZELNUT TWISTS

Total Time: 3 hours 30 minutes | Prep Time: 3 hours | Cook Time: 30 minutes

Ingredients:

1 cup whole milk, warmed to about 110°F (43°C)	1/4 cup granulated sugar
2 1/4 teaspoons active dry yeast	1/2 cup unsalted butter, melted
3 1/2 cups all-purpose flour	1/2 teaspoon salt
1/3 cup Nutella or chocolate hazelnut spread	1/2 cup chopped hazelnuts
1 egg, beaten (for egg wash)	Powdered sugar for dusting (optional)

Directions:

(1) Milk, sugar, and yeast should be cooked in the bread machine pan. Give it 5-10 minutes to foam. *(2)* Put butter, flour, and salt in a pan. Select the bread machine dough option and start. *(3)* After rising, place the dough on a lightly floured surface. Divide dough into 4 equal pieces. *(4)* Roll each piece into a 1/4-inch rectangle. *(5)* After evenly spreading Nutella, leave a slight gap around each square. Sprinkle chopped hazelnuts on Nutella. *(6)* Roll each rectangle tightly into a log from the long side. When chopped in half, one log end should remain intact. *(7)* Form a ring by twisting dough halves. Pinch ends to seal. *(8)* Before placing the twists on top, line a baking sheet with parchment paper. Cover it with a clean dishcloth and gently care for it for 30 to 45 minutes. *(9)* Preheat oven to 350°F (175°C). Sprinkle egg wash on twists. *(10)* Roast till golden, 25–30 minutes. Cool on a wire rack after baking. *(11)* Sprinkle powdered sugar before serving. Enjoy Chocolate Hazelnut Twists!

RASPBERRY ALMOND TWISTS

Total Time: 3 hours 30 minutes | Prep Time: 3 hours | Cook Time: 30 minutes

Ingredients:

1 cup whole milk, warmed to about 110°F (43°C)	1/4 cup granulated sugar
2 1/4 teaspoons active dry yeast	1/2 cup unsalted butter, melted
3 1/2 cups all-purpose flour	1/2 teaspoon salt
1/3 cup raspberry jam	1/2 cup sliced almonds

1 egg, beaten (for egg wash)	Powdered sugar for dusting (optional)

Directions:

(1) The bread machine pan needs hot milk, sugar, and yeast. Foam for 5-10 minutes. *(2)* Butter, flour, and salt in a pan. Set your bread machine to dough and start. *(3)* Post-rising, place the dough on a lightly floured surface. Split the dough into four equal pieces. *(4)* Roll pieces into 1/4-inch rectangles. *(5)* Spread raspberry jam evenly across rectangles with a small margin. Jam with almond slices. *(6)* From the long side, tightly roll each rectangle into a log. Every log should have one end intact when sliced in half. *(7)* Twist dough halves into rings. Seal ends by pinching. *(8)* Place twists on a parchment-lined baking sheet. Allow to rise for 30–45 minutes under a clean kitchen towel. *(9)* Start oven at 350°F (175°C). Coat twists in egg. *(10)* Roast for 25–30 minutes till browned. Cool baked goods on a wire rack. *(11)* Sugar before serving is optional. Enjoy raspberry almond twists!

LEMON CREAM CHEESE TWISTS

Total Time: 3 hours 30 minutes | Prep Time: 3 hours | Cook Time: 30 minutes

Ingredients:

1 cup whole milk, warmed to about 110°F (43°C)	1/4 cup granulated sugar
2 1/4 teaspoons active dry yeast	1/2 cup unsalted butter, melted
3 1/2 cups all-purpose flour	1/2 teaspoon salt
1/3 cup lemon curd	4 ounces cream cheese, softened
1 egg, beaten (for egg wash)	Powdered sugar for dusting (optional)

Directions:

(1) The bread machine pan needs hot milk, sugar, and yeast. Foam for 5-10 minutes. *(2)* Butter, flour, and salt in a pan. Set your bread machine to dough and start. *(3)* Post-rising, place the dough on a lightly floured surface. Split the dough into four equal pieces. *(4)* Roll pieces into 1/4-inch rectangles. *(5)* Smoothen softened cream cheese and lemon curd in a small bowl. Put ingredients on each rectangle evenly. *(6)*

From the long side, tightly roll each rectangle into a log. Every log should have one end intact when sliced in half. (7) Twist dough halves into rings. Seal ends by pinching. (8) Place twists on a parchment-lined baking sheet. Allow to rise for 30–45 minutes under a clean kitchen towel. (9) Start oven at 350°F (175°C). Coat twists in egg. (10) Roast for 25–30 minutes till browned. Cool baked goods on a wire rack. (11) Sugar before serving is optional. Lemon Cream Cheese Twists!

ORANGE CRANBERRY TWISTS

Total Time: 3 hours 30 minutes | Prep Time: 3 hours | Cook Time: 30 minutes

Ingredients:

1 cup whole milk, warmed to about 110°F (43°C)	1/4 cup granulated sugar
2 1/4 teaspoons active dry yeast	1/2 cup unsalted butter, melted
3 1/2 cups all-purpose flour	1/2 teaspoon salt
1/3 cup orange marmalade	1/2 cup dried cranberries
1 egg, beaten (for egg wash)	Powdered sugar for dusting (optional)

Directions:

(1) The bread machine pan needs hot milk, sugar, and yeast. Foam for 5-10 minutes. (2) Butter, flour, and salt in a pan. Set your bread machine to dough and start. (3) Post-rising, place the dough on a lightly floured surface. Split the dough into four equal pieces. (4) Roll pieces into 1/4-inch rectangles. (5) Spread orange marmalade evenly on rectangles with a small margin. Marmalade with dried cranberries. (6) From the long side, tightly roll each rectangle into a log. Every log should have one end intact when sliced in half. (7) Twist dough halves into rings. Seal ends by pinching. (8) Place twists on a parchment-lined baking sheet. Allow to rise for 30–45 minutes under a clean kitchen towel. (9) Start oven at 350°F (175°C). Coat twists in egg. (10) Roast for 25–30 minutes till browned. Cool baked goods on a wire rack. (11) Sugar before serving is optional. Try Orange Cranberry Twists!

SPINACH AND CHEESE TWISTS

Total Time: 3 hours 30 minutes | Prep Time: 3 hours | Cook Time: 30 minutes

Ingredients:

1 cup whole milk, warmed to about 43°C	1/4 cup granulated sugar
2 1/4 teaspoons active dry yeast	1/2 cup unsalted butter, melted
3 1/2 cups all-purpose flour	1/2 teaspoon salt
1 cup cooked spinach, squeezed dry and chopped	1 cup shredded mozzarella cheese
1 egg, beaten (for egg wash)	Powdered sugar for dusting (optional)

Directions:

(1) Milk, sugar, and yeast should be cooked in the bread machine pan. Give it 5-10 minutes to foam. (2) Put butter, flour, and salt in a pan. Select the bread machine dough option and start. (3) After rising, place the dough on a lightly floured surface. Divide dough into 4 equal pieces. (4) Roll each piece into a 1/4-inch rectangle. (5) On each rectangle, sprinkle chopped spinach and mozzarella. (6) Roll each rectangle tightly into a log from the long side. When chopped in half, one log end should remain intact. (7) Form a ring by twisting dough halves. Pinch ends to seal. (8) On a parchment-lined baking sheet, arrange twists. Let it rise for 30–45 minutes, covered with a clean kitchen towel. (9) Preheat oven to 350°F (175°C). Sprinkle egg wash on twists. (10) Roast till golden, 25–30 minutes. Cool on a wire rack after baking. (11) Sprinkle powdered sugar before serving. Cheese and spinach twists!

SUN-DRIED TOMATO PESTO TWISTS

Total Time: 2 hours 30 minutes | Prep Time: 2 hours | Yield: 12 twists

Ingredients:

1 cup warm water	2 tablespoons olive oil
3 cups bread flour	2 teaspoons sugar
1 teaspoon salt	2 1/4 teaspoons active dry yeast
1/2 cup sun-dried tomatoes, chopped	1/4 cup store-bought or homemade pesto

1/4 cup grated
Parmesan cheese

Directions:

(1) According to the manufacturer, mix warm water, olive oil, bread flour, sugar, salt, and yeast in the bread machine pan. *(2)* Pick the dough cycle and start. *(3)* Put the dough on a floured surface after the dough cycle. Be patient for 10 minutes. *(4)* Heat oven to 375°F (190°C). Baking sheet with parchment. *(5)* Roll out the dough into a large 1/4-inch rectangle. *(6)* Cover the dough with pesto, leaving a little border. *(7)* Sprinkle pesto with chopped sun-dried tomatoes and Parmesan. *(8)* Make a tight log of dough from one long side. *(9)* Divide the log into 12 equal pieces with a sharp knife. *(10)* Twist and set each dough piece on the baking sheet. *(11)* Bake twists till golden brown in preheated oven for 20–25 minutes. *(12)* SERVE after cooling slightly from the oven. Enjoy Sun-Dried Tomato Pesto Twists!

CHEDDAR BACON TWISTS

Total Time: 3 hours | Prep Time: 2 hours 30 minutes | Yield: 12 twists

Ingredients:

1 cup warm milk	2 tablespoons unsalted butter, melted
3 cups bread flour	2 teaspoons sugar
1 teaspoon salt	2 1/4 teaspoons active dry yeast
1 cup shredded cheddar cheese	6 slices cooked bacon, crumbled
2 tablespoons chopped chives	

Directions:

(1) According to the manufacturer, mix warm milk, melted butter, bread flour, sugar, salt, and yeast in the bread machine pan. *(2)* Pick the dough cycle and start. *(3)* Put the dough on a floured surface after the dough cycle. Be patient for 10 minutes. *(4)* Heat oven to 375°F (190°C). Baking sheet with parchment. *(5)* Roll out the dough into a large 1/4-inch rectangle. *(6)* On dough, equally distribute shredded cheddar cheese, crumbled bacon, and chopped chives. *(7)*

Carefully push toppings into the dough. *(8)* Separate the dough into 12 equal pieces using a pizza cutter or sharp knife. *(9)* Twist and place each dough strip on the baking sheet. *(10)* Cook the twists till golden brown and the cheese is melted and bubbling in the preheated oven for 25–30 minutes. *(11)* SERVE after cooling slightly from the oven. Enjoy cheddar bacon twists!

ASIAGO GARLIC TWISTS

Total Time: 2 hours 30 minutes | Prep Time: 2 hours | Yield: 12 twists

Ingredients:

1 cup warm water	2 tablespoons olive oil
3 cups bread flour	2 teaspoons sugar
1 teaspoon salt	2 teaspoons active dry yeast
1 cup shredded Asiago cheese	2 tablespoons minced garlic
2 tablespoons chopped fresh parsley	1/4 cup melted butter

Directions:

(1) In the bread machine pan, mix warm water, olive oil, flour, sugar, salt, and yeast. Choose the dough cycle and start. *(2)* Transfer the dough to a floured surface and divide it into 12 equal pieces after the dough cycle. Make 10-inch ropes from each piece. *(3)* Preheat oven to 375°F (190°C). Roll parchment paper on a baking pan. *(4)* Create spirals from each rope and arrange them on the baking sheet with space between them. *(5)* Mix minced garlic, chopped parsley, and shredded Asiago cheese in a small bowl. Dip each twist in melted butter and top with Asiago. *(6)* Brown and finish cooking in a preheated oven, stirring once or twice. This should take around 15 to 20 minutes. After baking, let cool before serving. Eat these Asiago Garlic Twists warm!

HAM AND SWISS TWISTS

Total Time: 3 hours | Prep Time: 2 hours 30 minutes | Yield: 12 twists

Ingredients:

1 cup warm milk	2 tablespoons melted butter

3 cups bread flour	2 tablespoons sugar
1 teaspoon salt	2 teaspoons active dry yeast
1 cup diced ham	1 cup shredded Swiss cheese
1/4 cup Dijon mustard	

Directions:

(1) In the bread machine pan, mix warm milk, melted butter, flour, sugar, salt, and yeast. Choose the dough cycle and start. **(2)** Transfer the dough to a floured surface and divide it into 12 equal pieces after the dough cycle. Make 10-inch ropes from each piece. **(3)** Preheat oven to 375°F (190°C). Roll parchment paper on a baking pan. **(4)** Create spirals from each rope and arrange them on the baking sheet with space between them. **(5)** In a small bowl, mix chopped ham, shredded Swiss cheese, and Dijon mustard. Spread mixture on twists. **(6)** To get a golden brown hue and ensure that it is cooked through, cook in a preheated oven for 20 to 25 minutes. **(7)** After baking, let cool before serving. Delicious Ham and Swiss Twists make a great appetizer or snack!

PARMESAN HERB TWISTS

Total Time: 2 hours 45 minutes | Prep Time: 2 hours 15 minutes | Yield: 12 twists

Ingredients:

1 cup warm water	2 tablespoons olive oil
3 cups bread flour	2 tablespoons grated Parmesan cheese
1 tablespoon dried Italian herbs	1 teaspoon garlic powder
2 teaspoons active dry yeast	1/4 cup melted butter
Additional grated Parmesan cheese for topping	

Directions:

(1) Blend warm water, olive oil, bread flour, grated Parmesan cheese, dried Italian herbs, garlic powder, and yeast in the bread machine pan. Choose the dough cycle and start. **(2)** After the dough cycle, split it into 12 equal pieces on a floured surface. Each piece becomes a 10-inch rope. **(3)** Heat oven to 375°F (190°C). Baking sheet with parchment. **(4)** Put each rope on the baking sheet in a spiral with room between twists. **(5)** Top each twist with grated Parmesan cheese and melted butter. **(6)** Cook in a preheated oven for fifteen to twenty minutes or until cooked through and a golden brown color. **(7)** SERVE after cooling slightly from the oven. Tasteful Parmesan Herb Twists add flavor to any meal!

ONION DILL TWISTS

Total Time: 3 hours 30 minutes | Prep Time: 15 minutes | Yield: 12 twists

Ingredients:

1 cup warm water	2 tablespoons olive oil
3 cups bread flour	2 tablespoons sugar
1 1/2 teaspoons salt	2 teaspoons dried dill
1 tablespoon dried minced onion	2 1/4 teaspoons active dry yeast

Directions:

(1) Follow the manufacturer-recommended sequence when adding ingredients to the bread machine pan. **(2)** Turn on the dough cycle and press the start button. **(3)** Take the dough out of the machine when the dough cycle is finished and divide it into 12 equal portions. **(4)** Make a 12-inch-long rope out of each piece. **(5)** After that, shape or knot each rope as you like, and set it on a baking sheet that has been buttered. **(6)** Wrap in a damp kitchen towel and set aside to rise for around half an hour or until doubled in size. **(7)** Turn the oven on high heat (375°F, 190°C). **(8)** After 12–15 minutes in the oven, the twists should be golden brown. **(9)** Graze when hot and savor!

ROSEMARY OLIVE TWISTS

Total Time: 3 hours 30 minutes | Prep Time: 15 minutes

Ingredients:

1 cup warm water	2 tablespoons olive oil
3 cups bread flour	1 tablespoon sugar
2 teaspoons salt	2 teaspoons active dry yeast
1/2 cup chopped Kalamata olives	2 tablespoons chopped fresh rosemary

Directions:

(1) The manufacturer recommends placing all ingredients except olives and rosemary in the bread machine pan in order. *(2)* Start the Dough cycle. *(3)* Remove the dough from the machine and place it on a lightly floured board after the cycle. *(4)* Knead chopped olives and rosemary gently until equally distributed. *(5)* Roll 12 equal chunks of dough into 10-inch ropes. *(6)* After you've spiralized each rope, set it on a baking sheet lined with paper. *(7)* After half an hour, place it in a warm place and cover it with a clean kitchen towel to let it rise. Heat the oven to 190°C. *(8)* Bake twists until golden brown, 20–25 minutes. *(9)* Cool gently before serving.

EVERYTHING BAGEL TWISTS

Total Time: 3 hours 30 minutes | Prep Time: 15 minutes | Yield: 8 twists

Ingredients:

1 cup warm water	2 tablespoons olive oil
3 cups bread flour	2 tablespoons sugar
1 1/2 teaspoons salt	1 tablespoon active dry yeast
2 tablespoons everything bagel seasoning	

Directions:

(1) As directed by the manufacturer, add all ingredients—aside from the everything bagel seasoning—to the bread machine pan in the specified order. *(2)* After choosing the dough cycle, turn on the machine. *(3)* After the dough cycle is finished, take the dough out of the machine and split it into eight equal pieces. *(4)* Each part should be rolled into a 12-inch-long rope. *(5)* Roll each rope into a pretzel shape, then arrange on a baking sheet covered with paper. *(6)* Turn the oven on to 190°C. *(7)* After giving each twist a quick wipe with water, season with everything bagel. *(8)* Roast for 15 to 20 minutes or until browned on top. *(9)* Before serving, let the twists cool slightly. Have fun!

CINNAMON SUGAR TWISTS

Total Time: 3 hours 15 minutes | Prep Time: 10 minutes | Yield: 8 twists

Ingredients:

1 cup warm milk	2 tablespoons butter, melted
3 cups bread flour	2 tablespoons sugar
1 teaspoon salt	1 tablespoon active dry yeast
1/4 cup granulated sugar	2 teaspoons ground cinnamon

Directions:

(1) In the sequence suggested by the manufacturer, add warm milk, melted butter, bread flour, sugar, salt, and yeast to the bread machine pan. *(2)* After choosing the dough cycle, turn on the machine. *(3)* When the dough is finished, separate it into eight equal pieces. *(4)* Each part should be rolled into a 12-inch-long rope. *(5)* After you've twisted each rope, place it on a parchment-lined baking sheet. *(6)* Turn the oven on to 190°C. *(7)* Grated sugar and ground cinnamon should be mixed together in a small bowl. *(8)* After giving each twist a quick water spray, liberally dust them with the cinnamon-sugar mixture. *(9)* Bake until gently browned, 15 to 20 minutes. *(10)* Before serving, let the twists cool slightly. Have fun!

SESAME SEED TWISTS

Total Time: 3 hours 30 minutes | Prep Time: 15 minutes | Yield: 8 twists

Ingredients:

1 cup warm water	2 tablespoons olive oil
3 cups bread flour	2 tablespoons sugar
1 1/2 teaspoons salt	1 tablespoon active dry yeast
1/4 cup sesame seeds	

Directions:

(1) As directed by the manufacturer, fill the bread machine pan with warm water, olive oil, bread flour, sugar, salt, and yeast. *(2)* Turn on the dough cycle and begin operating the machine. *(3)* After the dough is prepared, split it into eight equal pieces. *(4)* Create a 12-inch-long rope out of each section. *(5)* A twist form is formed out of each rope and arranged on a baking sheet covered with parchment paper. *(6)* Set oven temperature

to 190°C. *(7)* Lightly moisten each twist with water and liberally dust with sesame seeds. *(8)* Allow fifteen to twenty minutes for baking until a golden brown color develops. *(9)* When ready to serve, let the twists cool somewhat. Enjoy yourself!

GARLIC PARMESAN WREATH BREAD

Total Time: 3 hours 45 minutes | Prep Time: 15 minutes | Yield: 1 loaf

Ingredients:

1 cup warm water	2 tablespoons olive oil
3 cups bread flour	2 teaspoons sugar
1 1/2 teaspoons salt	2 teaspoons active dry yeast
1/4 cup grated Parmesan cheese	2 cloves garlic, minced
1 tablespoon dried parsley	

Directions:

(1) In the bread machine pan, add olive oil and warm water. *(2)* Before adding yeast, sugar, salt, and flour to the pan, follow the manufacturer's instructions in that order. *(3)* Turn the machine on and choose the dough cycle. *(4)* Scrape the dough out of the bread machine and give it a little kneading in flour. *(5)* Roll the dough into a rectangle. *(6)* Parmesan, minced garlic, and dried parsley should be uniformly distributed on the dough. *(7)* Form a wreath by tightly rolling the dough from the long side. *(8)* Rise the wreath on a greased baking sheet for 30 minutes in a warm location. *(9)* Heat the oven to 190°C. *(10)* Bake wreath bread till golden brown, 25–30 minutes. *(11)* Slicing and serving after a minor cooling. Eat your Garlic Parmesan Wreath Bread!

HERB AND CHEESE WREATH BREAD

Total Time: 3 hours 30 minutes | Prep Time: 20 minutes

Ingredients:

1 cup warm water	2 tablespoons olive oil
3 cups bread flour	2 teaspoons sugar
1 teaspoon salt	2 teaspoons dried mixed herbs (such as oregano, thyme, and rosemary)

1 cup shredded mozzarella cheese
Additional olive oil for brushing

2 teaspoons active dry yeast

Directions:

(1) As directed by the manufacturer, mix warm water, olive oil, bread flour, sugar, salt, herbs, cheese, and yeast in the bread machine pan. *(2)* Select and start the dough cycle. *(3)* Remove the dough from the machine and set it on a lightly floured surface. Make small, equal-sized dough balls. *(4)* Arrange the dough balls into a wreath shape in a prepared circular cake pan. Put a clean kitchen towel over the dough and let it rise for 30 minutes in a warm place. *(5)* Heat the oven to 190°C. *(6)* Brush olive oil on rising wreath bread. *(7)* Preheat oven and bake for 25-30 minutes till golden brown. *(8)* Cool the bread before serving. Savor warm!

SPINACH AND FETA WREATH BREAD

Total Time: 3 hours | Prep Time: 20 minutes | Yield: 1 loaf

Ingredients:

1 cup warm water	2 tablespoons olive oil
3 cups bread flour	2 tablespoons sugar
1 teaspoon salt	2 teaspoons active dry yeast
1 cup chopped fresh spinach	1/2 cup crumbled feta cheese
2 tablespoons finely chopped red onion	1 teaspoon garlic powder
1/2 teaspoon dried oregano	

Directions:

(1) Warm water and olive oil in the bread machine pan. *(2)* Use the manufacturer's sequence to add bread flour, sugar, salt, and yeast to the pan. *(3)* Start the machine on the dough. *(4)* Place the dough on a lightly floured board after removing it from the machine. Heat oven to 375°F (190°C). *(5)* Form a 12x16-inch rectangle from the dough. *(6)* Sprinkle crumbled feta, minced red onion, garlic powder, and dry oregano over dough. *(7)* Starting from a longer edge, tightly roll the dough into a log. *(8)* Move the dough log to a prepared baking sheet and

shape it into a wreath by linking the ends. **(9)** Bake until the bread is golden brown and hollow when tapped, 25–30 minutes. **(10)** After cooling, slice and serve the bread.

SUN-DRIED TOMATO PESTO WREATH BREAD

Total Time: 3 hours 30 minutes | Prep Time: 20 minutes | Yield: 1 loaf

Ingredients:

1 cup warm water	2 tablespoons olive oil
3 cups bread flour	2 tablespoons sugar
1 teaspoon salt	2 teaspoons active dry yeast
1/4 cup sun-dried tomato pesto	1/4 cup chopped sun-dried tomatoes
1/4 cup grated Parmesan cheese	1 tablespoon dried basil
1 egg, beaten (for egg wash)	

Directions:

(1) Warm water and olive oil in the bread machine pan. **(2)** Use the manufacturer's sequence to add bread flour, sugar, salt, and yeast to the pan. **(3)** Pick the dough cycle and start. **(4)** Take the dough out of the machine and give it a good smack. Form a 12x18-inch rectangle from the dough on a floured surface. **(5)** Spread sun-dried tomato pesto on dough. **(6)** Add chopped sun-dried tomatoes, Parmesan, and dry basil to pesto. **(7)** Start from a long side and tightly roll the dough. **(8)** Pinch the seam to seal and log. **(9)** Grease a baking sheet and form a dough ring with joined ends. **(10)** Let it sit for 30 minutes in a warm spot, covered with a moist dish towel. **(11)** Heat oven to 375°F (190°C). **(12)** Brush egg wash on the rising dough. **(13)** Bake till golden, 25–30 minutes. **(14)** Wait to slice and serve after cooling from the oven.

CHEDDAR BACON WREATH BREAD

Total Time: 3 hours 45 minutes | Prep Time: 25 minutes | Yield: 1 loaf

Ingredients:

1 cup warm milk	2 tablespoons butter, melted
3 cups bread flour	2 tablespoons sugar
1 teaspoon salt	2 teaspoons active dry yeast
1 cup shredded cheddar cheese	1/2 cup cooked and crumbled bacon
1/4 cup chopped green onions	1 tablespoon garlic powder
1 egg, beaten (for egg wash)	

Directions:

(1) Melt butter and warm milk in the bread machine pan. **(2)** The manufacturer recommends adding bread flour, sugar, salt, and yeast to the pan in order. **(3)** Select the dough cycle and start the machinery. **(4)** Take the dough out of the machine and punch it down. **(5)** Roll dough into a 12x18-inch rectangle on a floured surface. **(6)** Evenly sprinkle dough with shredded cheddar, crumbled bacon, chopped green onions, and garlic powder. **(7)** Roll the dough tightly from the long side. **(8)** Seal and log the seam with a pinch. **(9)** Form a dough ring on a greased baking sheet and connect the ends. **(10)** Let rise for 45 minutes in a warm location under a clean kitchen towel. **(11)** Preheat oven to 375°F (190°C). **(12)** Wash rising dough with beaten egg. **(13)** Bake until golden brown and 190°F (88°C) inside about 30–35 minutes. **(14)** Slice and serve after cooling from the oven.

ASIAGO GARLIC WREATH BREAD

Total Time: 3 hours 30 minutes | Prep Time: 20 minutes

Ingredients:

1 cup warm water	2 tablespoons olive oil
3 cups bread flour	2 tablespoons sugar
1 teaspoon salt	2 teaspoons active dry yeast
1 cup grated Asiago cheese	2 cloves garlic, minced
2 tablespoons chopped fresh parsley	Additional olive oil for brushing

Directions:

(1) Warm water and olive oil in the bread machine pan. **(2)** Use the manufacturer's sequence to add bread flour, sugar, salt, and yeast to the pan. **(3)** Pick the dough cycle and start. *(4)* Put the dough on a lightly floured surface after the dough cycle. *(5)* Mix the grated Asiago cheese, minced garlic, and chopped parsley into the dough after punching it down. *(6)* Roll small amounts of dough into 12-inch ropes. *(7)* Put the ropes in a wreath on a parchment-lined baking sheet, overlapping and linking the ends to form a circular. *(8)* Place the dough in a warm place with a clean kitchen towel for 30 minutes to rise. *(9)* Heat oven to 375°F (190°C). *(10)* Olive oil the risen dough. *(11)* The bread should be baked for 20 to 25 minutes while the oven is preheating or until it becomes brown and sounds hollow when tapped. *(12)* Let bread cool before serving. Enjoy!

HAM AND SWISS WREATH BREAD

Total Time: 3 hours 30 minutes | Prep Time: 15 minutes | Yields: 1 wreath loaf

Ingredients:

1 cup warm water	2 tablespoons olive oil
3 cups bread flour	1 tablespoon sugar
1 teaspoon salt	2 1/4 teaspoons active dry yeast
1/2 cup diced ham	1/2 cup shredded Swiss cheese
1/4 cup chopped fresh parsley	1/4 cup chopped green onions
1 egg, beaten (for egg wash)	Sesame seeds (optional, for garnish)

Directions:

(1) Warm water and olive oil in the bread machine pan. *(2)* Combine bread flour, sugar, salt, and yeast in the pan. *(3)* Choose the dough cycle and start. *(4)* After the dough cycle, remove it from the machine and flour it lightly. *(5)* Turn on the oven to 175°C. *(6)* Form a 12x18-inch rectangle from the dough. *(7)* On dough, evenly distribute diced ham, Swiss cheese, parsley, and green onions. *(8)* Shape the dough into a log by rolling it firmly from the longest side to the shortest. *(9)* Form the dough log into a circle, seam side down, on a prepared baking sheet. *(10)* Let it sit for 30 minutes in a warm spot, covered with a moist dish towel. *(11)* Pour beaten egg on rising dough and sprinkle sesame seeds if desired. *(12)* Bake 25-30 minutes till golden

brown in preheated oven. *(13)* After baking, let it cool before slicing. Enjoy hot!

THREE CHEESE WREATH BREAD

Total Time: 3 hours 45 minutes | Prep Time: 30 minutes | Yields: 1 wreath loaf

Ingredients:

1 cup warm milk	2 tablespoons unsalted butter, melted
3 cups bread flour	1 tablespoon sugar
1 teaspoon salt	2 1/4 teaspoons active dry yeast
1/2 cup shredded cheddar cheese	1/2 cup shredded mozzarella cheese
1/2 cup grated Parmesan cheese	1/4 cup chopped fresh basil
1/4 cup chopped sun-dried tomatoes	1 egg, beaten (for egg wash)
Italian seasoning (optional for garnish)	

Directions:

(1) Melt butter and warm milk in the bread machine pan. *(2)* Add bread flour, sugar, salt, and yeast to the pan in order. *(3)* Choose the dough cycle and start. *(4)* After the dough cycle finishes, take it out of the machine and set it on a surface that has been lightly dusted with flour. Preheat oven to 350°F (175°C). *(5)* Roll dough into a 12x18-inch rectangle. *(6)* Evenly sprinkle shredded cheddar, mozzarella, Parmesan, basil, and sun-dried tomatoes on the dough. *(7)* Form the dough into a log by rolling it tightly from one long edge to the other. *(8)* Form a circle on a prepared baking sheet with the dough log seam side down. *(9)* Let rise for 45 minutes in a warm location under a clean kitchen towel. *(10)* Brush rising dough with beaten egg and add Italian spice if desired. *(11)* Bake 30-35 minutes till golden brown in preheated oven. *(12)* Wait to slice after cooling from the oven. Warm-up!

ARTICHOKE AND PARMESAN WREATH BREAD

Total Time: 4 hours | Prep Time: 45 minutes | Yields: 1 wreath loaf

Ingredients:

1 cup warm water	2 tablespoons olive oil
3 cups bread flour	1 tablespoon sugar
1 teaspoon salt	2 1/4 teaspoons active dry yeast
1/2 cup chopped marinated artichoke hearts	1/2 cup grated Parmesan cheese
1/4 cup chopped fresh parsley	1/4 cup chopped green onions
1 egg, beaten (for egg wash)	Garlic powder (optional, for garnish)

Directions:

(1) Warm water and olive oil in the bread machine pan. *(2)* Combine bread flour, sugar, salt, and yeast in the pan. *(3)* Choose the dough cycle and start. *(4)* After the dough cycle, remove it from the machine and flour it lightly. *(5)* Turn on the oven to 175°C. *(6)* Form a 12x18-inch rectangle from the dough. *(7)* On dough, evenly distribute chopped marinated artichoke hearts, grated Parmesan, parsley, and green onions. *(8)* Construct a log shape by rolling the dough firmly, beginning at one long edge. *(9)* Place the dough log, seam side down, on a baking sheet that has been prepared and shapes it into a circle. *(10)* For the first hour, cover it with a clean dish towel and set it aside in a warm place to rise. *(11)* Egg-brush the risen dough and apply garlic powder if desired. *(12)* Bake till golden brown in preheated oven for 35-40 minutes. *(13)* After baking, let it cool before slicing. Enjoy hot!

TOMATO AND BASIL WREATH BREAD

Total Time: 3 hours 30 minutes | Prep Time: 15 minutes | Servings: 1 loaf

Ingredients:

1 cup warm water	2 tablespoons olive oil
3 cups bread flour	2 tablespoons sugar
1 teaspoon salt	2 teaspoons active dry yeast
1/2 cup sun-dried tomatoes, chopped	1/4 cup fresh basil leaves, chopped
1/4 cup grated Parmesan cheese	

Directions:

(1) In the sequence advised by the manufacturer, add warm water, olive oil, bread flour, sugar, salt, and yeast to your Zojirushi bread machine bread pan. *(2)* Start the "Dough" cycle. *(3)* Turn the bread machine off and transfer the dough to a board that has been lightly dusted with flour. Crumble the sun-dried tomatoes, add the basil, and mix in the Parmesan cheese after punching down the dough. *(4)* Roll 12 equal balls from the dough. *(5)* Place dough balls in a circle on a prepared baking sheet, touching each other to make a wreath. *(6)* Thirty minutes beneath a clean kitchen towel in a warm place will let the dough rise. *(7)* Heat the oven to 190°C. *(8)* The wreath bread should be golden brown and cooked through after 20–25 minutes in the preheated oven. *(9)* Cool the bread before serving. Savour your Tomato and Basil Wreath Bread!

SUN-DRIED TOMATO AND OLIVE WREATH BREAD

Total Time: 3 hours 30 minutes | Prep Time: 20 minutes | Servings: 8

Ingredients:

1 cup warm water	2 tablespoons olive oil
3 cups bread flour	2 tablespoons sugar
1 teaspoon salt	2 1/4 teaspoons active dry yeast
1/2 cup sun-dried tomatoes, chopped	1/4 cup black olives, sliced
2 tablespoons chopped fresh basil	1 tablespoon chopped fresh rosemary

Directions:

(1) Warm water and olive oil in the bread machine pan. *(2)* In the sequence indicated by the maker, add bread flour, sugar, salt, and yeast. *(3)* Choose the dough cycle and start. *(4)* After the cycle, take the dough and flour it. *(5)* Mix sun-dried tomatoes, black olives, basil, and rosemary into the dough after punching it down. *(6)* Create 16 balls from the dough. *(7)* Spread the balls on a prepared baking sheet in a circle with space between them. *(8)* Raise in a warm place for 30 minutes after covering with a clean kitchen towel. *(9)* Heat oven to 375°F (190°C). *(10)* Bake

till golden, 20–25 minutes. **(11)** SERVE after cooling slightly from the oven. Enjoy!

GARLIC AND HERB WREATH BREAD

Total Time: 3 hours 30 minutes | Prep Time: 15 minutes | Makes: 1 loaf

Ingredients:

1 cup warm water	2 tablespoons olive oil
3 cups bread flour	2 tablespoons sugar
1 teaspoon salt	Two teaspoons active dry yeast
3 cloves garlic, minced	2 tablespoons finely chopped fresh herbs

Directions:

(1) Olive oil and warm water should be combined in the bread machine pan. **(2)** In the pan, add the yeast, sugar, salt, and bread flour in that order. **(3)** After you've chosen the dough setting on your bread machine, press the start button. **(4)** After the dough cycle is finished, take the dough out of the machine and transfer it to a surface that has been lightly dusted. **(5)** Turn the oven on to 190°C. **(6)** The dough should be rolled into a rectangle. **(7)** Evenly distribute chopped herbs and minced garlic over the dough. **(8)** After you've rolled the dough into a log shape, pinch its ends to seal it like a wreath. **(9)** Allow the wreath to rise in a warm place for half an hour after placing it on an oiled baking sheet. **(10)** To get a golden brown color, bake for 20 to 30 minutes. **(11)** Make sure the bread has cooled down a bit before you serve it.

PESTO AND PINE NUT WREATH BREAD

Total Time: 3 hours | Prep Time: 20 minutes | Yields: 1 loaf

Ingredients:

1 cup warm water	2 tablespoons olive oil
3 cups bread flour	2 tablespoons sugar
1 teaspoon salt	2 1/4 teaspoons active dry yeast
1/4 cup prepared pesto	1/4 cup pine nuts, toasted
1 egg, beaten (for egg wash)	

Directions:

(1) As advised by the manufacturer, mix warm water, olive oil, bread flour, sugar, salt, and yeast in the bread machine pan. **(2)** Turn the machine on and choose the dough cycle. **(3)** Punch down the dough after removing it from the mixer. Make two equal dough parts. **(4)** Roll each portion into an 18-inch rope. Form a circle with the ropes and squeeze the ends to seal. **(5)** Let the dough circle rise in a warm area for 30 minutes on a greased baking sheet covered with a clean kitchen towel. **(6)** Heat the oven to 190°C. Baste the rising dough with egg wash. **(7)** Spread pesto equally on dough and top with toasted pine nuts. **(8)** The bread should be golden brown and hollow when tapped after 20–25 minutes in the preheated oven. **(9)** Cool the bread before slicing and serving.

LEMON AND HERB WREATH BREAD

Total Time: 3 hours 15 minutes | Prep Time: 25 minutes | Yields: 1 loaf

Ingredients:

1 cup warm water	2 tablespoons olive oil
3 cups bread flour	2 tablespoons sugar
1 teaspoon salt	2 1/4 teaspoons active dry yeast
Zest of 1 lemon	2 tablespoons chopped fresh herbs
1 egg, beaten	

Directions:

(1) In the bread machine pan, add warm water, olive oil, bread flour, sugar, salt, lemon zest, herbs, and yeast in the manufacturer's sequence. **(2)** Select the dough cycle and start the machinery. **(3)** Take the dough out of the machine and punch it down. Two equal amounts of dough. **(4)** Make an 18-inch rope from each part. Pinching the ends seals the ropes in a circle. **(5)** The dough circle should rise in a warm environment for 30–35 minutes on a greased baking sheet covered with a clean kitchen towel. **(6)** Preheat oven to 375°F (190°C). Wash rising dough with beaten egg. **(7)** After 20–25 minutes in the preheated oven, the bread should be golden brown and hollow when tapped. **(8)** Slicing and serving require some bread cooling.

BLUE CHEESE AND WALNUT WREATH BREAD

Total Time: 3 hours 30 minutes | Prep Time: 30 minutes

Ingredients:

1 cup crumbled blue cheese	1/2 cup chopped walnuts
3 cups bread flour	1 1/2 teaspoons instant yeast
1 teaspoon salt	1 tablespoon sugar
1 cup warm water	2 tablespoons olive oil

Directions:

(1) Mix crumbled blue cheese and chopped walnuts in a small bowl. Set aside. *(2)* Add bread flour, instant yeast, salt, and sugar to the bread machine pan. *(3)* Add warm water and olive oil. *(4)* Choose "Dough" on your bread maker and push start. *(5)* Put the dough on a floured board after it comes out of the bread maker. *(6)* Roll the dough into a 1/4-inch rectangle. *(7)* Apply blue cheese and walnut mixture equally to the dough. *(8)* Tightly roll out the dough, beginning with the longest side. Pinch seams to seal. *(9)* Carefully place the rolled dough on a parchment-lined baking sheet. *(10)* Connect the dough ends to make a wreath. *(11)* Let the dough rise for 30 minutes under a clean kitchen towel. *(12)* Heat the oven to 190°C. *(13)* Bake the bread till golden brown, 25-30 minutes. *(14)* Cool the bread before slicing and serving. Eat Blue Cheese and Walnut Wreath Bread!

BACON AND CHEDDAR WREATH BREAD

Total Time: 3 hours 30 minutes | Prep Time: 30 minutes

Ingredients:

6 slices bacon, cooked and crumbled	1 cup shredded cheddar cheese
3 cups bread flour	1 1/2 teaspoons instant yeast
1 teaspoon salt	1 tablespoon sugar
1 cup warm water	2 tablespoons olive oil

Directions:

(1) After crisping, crush the bacon. Set aside. *(2)* Mix crumbled bacon and shredded cheddar cheese in a small bowl. Set aside. *(3)* Add bread flour, instant yeast, salt, and sugar to the bread machine pan. *(4)* Add warm water and olive oil. *(5)* Choose "Dough" on your bread maker and push start. *(6)* Put the dough on a floured board after it comes out of the bread maker. *(7)* Roll the dough into a 1/4-inch rectangle. *(8)* Sprinkle bacon and cheddar cheese equally on the dough. *(9)* Tightly roll out the dough, beginning with the longest side. *(10)* Pinch seams to seal. *(11)* Carefully place the rolled dough on a parchment-lined baking sheet. *(12)* Connect the dough ends to make a wreath. *(13)* Let the dough rise for 30 minutes under a clean kitchen towel. *(14)* Heat the oven to 190°C. *(15)* Bake the bread till golden brown, 25-30 minutes. *(16)* Cool the bread before slicing and serving. Eat Bacon and Cheddar Wreath Bread!

CARAMELIZED ONION AND GRUYERE WREATH BREAD

Total Time: 3 hours 30 minutes | Prep Time: 30 minutes

Ingredients:

2 large onions, thinly sliced	1 tablespoon olive oil
1 cup shredded Gruyere cheese	3 cups bread flour
1 1/2 teaspoons instant yeast	1 teaspoon salt
1 tablespoon sugar	1 cup warm water
2 tablespoons olive oil	

Directions:

(1) Cook olive oil in a skillet on medium. Add sliced onions and stir occasionally until caramelized, 20–25 minutes. Allow to cool. *(2)* Add bread flour, instant yeast, salt, and sugar to the bread machine pan. *(3)* Add warm water and olive oil. *(4)* Choose "Dough" on your bread maker and push start. *(5)* Put the dough on a floured board after it comes out of the bread maker. *(6)* Roll the dough into a 1/4-inch rectangle. *(7)* Cover the dough with caramelized onions and Gruyere cheese. *(8)* Tightly roll out the dough, beginning with the longest side. *(9)* Pinch seams to seal. *(10)* Carefully place the rolled dough on a parchment-lined baking sheet. *(11)* Connect the dough ends to make a wreath. *(12)* Let the dough rise for 30 minutes under a clean kitchen towel. *(13)* Heat the oven to 190°C.

(14) Bake the bread till golden brown, 25-30 minutes. **(15)** Cool the bread before slicing and serving. Eat Caramelized Onion and Gruyere Wreath Bread!

FIG AND GOAT CHEESE WREATH BREAD

Total Time: 3 hours 30 minutes | Prep Time: 30 minutes

Ingredients:

1/2 cup chopped dried figs	1/2 cup crumbled goat cheese
3 cups bread flour	1 1/2 teaspoons instant yeast
1 teaspoon salt	1 tablespoon sugar
1 cup warm water	2 tablespoons olive oil

Directions:

(1) Mix crumbled goat cheese and chopped dried figs in a small bowl. Save. **(2)** To the bread machine pan, add flour, instant yeast, salt, and sugar. **(3)** Put warm water and olive oil in. **(4)** Start your bread maker on "Dough" mode. **(5)** After taking the dough out of the bread machine, turn it out onto a floured board. **(6)** Roll dough into a 1/4-inch rectangle. **(7)** Sprinkle fig-goat cheese mixture over the dough evenly. **(8)** Roll the dough tightly from the long side. **(9)** Seal seams by pinching. **(10)** Carefully place the rolled dough on a baking sheet that has been prepared with paper. **(11)** Create a wreath out of dough and secure its ends. **(12)** Let the dough rise for half an hour, covered with a clean dish towel. **(13)** Preheat oven to 375°F (190°C). **(14)** Bake bread until golden brown, 25–30 minutes. **(15)** Slicing and serving require some bread cooling. Delight in Fig and Goat Cheese Wreath Bread!

HONEY AND WALNUT WREATH BREAD

Total Time: 3 hours 30 minutes | Prep Time: 30 minutes

Ingredients:

1/4 cup honey	1/2 cup chopped walnuts
3 cups bread flour	1 1/2 teaspoons instant yeast
1 teaspoon salt	1 tablespoon sugar
1 cup warm water	2 tablespoons olive oil

Directions:

(1) Mix chopped walnuts and honey in a small bowl. Set aside. **(2)** Add bread flour, instant yeast, salt, and sugar to the bread machine pan. **(3)** Add warm water and olive oil. **(4)** Choose "Dough" on your bread maker and push start. **(5)** Put the dough on a floured board after it comes out of the bread maker. **(6)** Roll the dough into a 1/4-inch rectangle. **(7)** Evenly drizzle the honey and walnut mixture over the dough. **(8)** Tightly roll out the dough, beginning with the longest side. Pinch seams to seal. **(9)** Carefully place the rolled dough on a parchment-lined baking sheet. **(10)** Connect the dough ends to make a wreath. **(11)** Let the dough rise for 30 minutes under a clean kitchen towel. **(12)** Heat the oven to 190°C. **(13)** Bake the bread till golden brown, 25-30 minutes. **(14)** Cool the bread before slicing and serving. Honey and Walnut Wreath Bread, enjoy!

CHOCOLATE CHIP ZUCCHINI BREAD

Total Time: 3 hours 15 minutes | Prep Time: 15 minutes | Yield: 1 loaf

Ingredients:

1 1/2 cups all-purpose flour	1/2 teaspoon baking powder
1/2 teaspoon baking soda	1/2 teaspoon salt
1 teaspoon ground cinnamon	1/2 teaspoon ground nutmeg
1 cup shredded zucchini, drained	1/2 cup granulated sugar
1/2 cup brown sugar	1/2 cup vegetable oil
2 large eggs	1 teaspoon vanilla extract
3/4 cup semisweet chocolate chips	

Directions:

(1) Zojirushi bread machines should be preheated as directed. **(2)** A medium-sized basin is ideal for whisking flour, baking soda, cinnamon, salt, and nutmeg. **(3)** Mix shredded zucchini, granulated sugar, brown sugar, vegetable oil, eggs, and vanilla in a large basin. Blend well. **(4)** Slowly add dry ingredients to wet components and whisk until incorporated. Do not overmix. **(5)** Fold chocolate chips into the batter until evenly distributed. **(6)** Put the batter in the bread machine pan. **(7)** Select "Quick

Bread" and choose crust color, then hit start. **(8)** Leave the loaf to rest in the pan for 10 minutes after carefully removing it from the bread machine. The last step in cooling is to set it on a wire rack. Cut and serve.

LEMON BLUEBERRY ZUCCHINI BREAD

Total Time: 3 hours 30 minutes | Prep Time: 20 minutes | Yield: 1 loaf

Ingredients:

1 1/2 cups all-purpose flour	1/2 teaspoon baking powder
1/2 teaspoon baking soda	1/2 teaspoon salt
Zest of 1 lemon	1 cup shredded zucchini, drained
1/2 cup granulated sugar	1/2 cup brown sugar
1/2 cup vegetable oil	2 large eggs
1 teaspoon vanilla extract	1 cup fresh or frozen blueberries

Directions:

(1) Zojirushi bread machines should be preheated as directed. **(2)** Mix flour, baking powder, soda, salt, and lemon zest in a medium bowl. **(3)** Mix shredded zucchini, granulated sugar, brown sugar, vegetable oil, eggs, and vanilla in a large basin. Blend well. **(4)** Slowly add dry ingredients to wet components and whisk until incorporated. Do not overmix. **(5)** Spread blueberries evenly in the batter by gently folding. **(6)** Put the batter in the bread machine pan. **(7)** Select "Quick Bread" and choose crust color, then hit start. **(8)** Take the loaf out of the bread machine with care and set it aside to rest for 10 minutes in the pan. After it's done, place it on a wire rack to cool completely. After slicing, serve.

PINEAPPLE COCONUT ZUCCHINI BREAD

Total Time: 3 hours 45 minutes | Prep Time: 25 minutes

Ingredients:

1 1/2 cups all-purpose flour	half a teaspoon of baking powder
1/2 teaspoon baking soda	1/2 teaspoon salt
1 teaspoon ground cinnamon	1 cup shredded zucchini, drained
1/2 cup granulated sugar	1/2 cup brown sugar
1/2 cup vegetable oil	2 large eggs
1 teaspoon vanilla extract	1/2 cup crushed pineapple, drained
1/2 cup shredded coconut	

Directions:

(1) Zojirushi bread machines should be preheated as directed. **(2)** Mix flour, baking powder, soda, salt, and cinnamon in a medium basin. **(3)** Mix shredded zucchini, granulated sugar, brown sugar, vegetable oil, eggs, and vanilla in a large basin. Blend well. **(4)** Slowly add dry ingredients to wet components and whisk until incorporated. Do not overmix. **(5)** Fold smashed pineapple and shredded coconut into batter until equally distributed. **(6)** Put the batter in the bread machine pan. **(7)** Select "Quick Bread" and choose crust color, then hit start. **(8)** After removing the loaf from the bread machine, carefully place it back in the pan and let it a 10-minute rest. Finally, to finish cooling, set it on a wire rack; before serving, slice.

CARROT ZUCCHINI BREAD

Total Time: 3 hours 30 minutes | Prep Time: 20 minutes | Yield: 1 loaf

Ingredients:

1 1/2 cups all-purpose flour	1/2 teaspoon baking powder
1/2 teaspoon baking soda	1/2 teaspoon salt
1 teaspoon ground cinnamon	1/2 cup shredded zucchini, drained
1/2 cup shredded carrots	1/2 cup granulated sugar
1/2 cup brown sugar	1/2 cup vegetable oil
2 large eggs	1 teaspoon vanilla extract
1/2 cup chopped walnuts (optional)	

Directions:

(1) Zojirushi bread machines should be preheated as directed. **(2)** Mix flour, baking powder, soda, salt, and cinnamon in a medium basin. **(3)** Mix the shredded zucchini, carrots, granulated sugar, brown sugar, vegetable oil, eggs, and vanilla essence in a large basin. Blend well. *(4)* Slowly add dry ingredients to wet components and whisk until incorporated. Do not overmix. *(5)* If using, evenly mix chopped walnuts into the batter. *(6)* Put the batter in the bread machine pan. *(7)* Select "Quick Bread" and choose crust color, then hit start. *(8)* Leave the loaf to rest in the pan for 10 minutes after carefully removing it from the bread machine. The last step in cooling is to set it on a wire rack. Cut and serve.

ALMOND ZUCCHINI BREAD

Total Time: 3 hours 15 minutes | Prep Time: 15 minutes | Yield: 1 loaf

Ingredients:

1 1/2 cups all-purpose flour	1/2 teaspoon baking powder
1/2 teaspoon baking soda	1/2 teaspoon salt
1/2 cup shredded zucchini, drained	1/2 cup granulated sugar
1/2 cup brown sugar	1/2 cup vegetable oil
2 large eggs	1 teaspoon almond extract
1/2 cup sliced almonds	

Directions:

(1) Following manufacturer instructions, preheat your Zojirushi bread machine. *(2)* In a medium basin, mix flour, baking powder, soda, and salt. *(3)* In a large bowl, mix shredded zucchini, granulated sugar, brown sugar, vegetable oil, eggs, and almond extract. Thoroughly mix. *(4)* Toss the dry ingredients into the liquid ones and stir until just combined. Be careful not to combine the ingredients too much. *(5)* Sliced almonds should be uniformly dispersed throughout the batter. *(6)* Put batter in bread machine pan. *(7)* Press start after selecting "Quick Bread" and the crust color. *(8)* The bread should be carefully removed from the bread machine and cooled in the pan for 10 minutes before being transferred to a wire rack to finish cooling. Slice, serve.

BANANA ZUCCHINI BREAD

Total Time: 3 hours | Prep Time: 15 minutes

Ingredients:

1 medium ripe banana, mashed	1 cup shredded zucchini
2 eggs	1/2 cup vegetable oil
1 teaspoon vanilla extract	1 1/2 cups all-purpose flour
1 cup granulated sugar	1 teaspoon baking powder
1/2 teaspoon baking soda	1/2 teaspoon salt
1 teaspoon ground cinnamon	

Directions:

(1) Set the Zojirushi bread maker to the Quick Bread setting and preheat it. *(2)* Beat together eggs, shredded zucchini, mashed banana, vegetable oil, and vanilla extract in a mixing dish. Blend thoroughly. *(3)* In a third dish, sift together the flour, sugar, baking powder, salt, and cinnamon. *(4)* Stir until just blended, and gradually add the dry ingredients to the wet components. Take caution not to blend too much. *(5)* After adding the batter, cover the bread machine pan. *(6)* Choose the Quick Bread option and hit the start button. *(7)* After the cycle is complete, gently transfer the bread to a wire rack to cool. Once cooled, slice and serve.

PUMPKIN ZUCCHINI BREAD

Total Time: 3 hours 30 minutes | Prep Time: 20 minutes

Ingredients:

1 cup canned pumpkin puree	1 cup shredded zucchini
2 eggs	1/2 cup vegetable oil
1 teaspoon vanilla extract	1 3/4 cups all-purpose flour
1 cup granulated sugar	1 teaspoon baking soda
1/2 teaspoon baking powder	1/2 teaspoon salt
1 teaspoon ground cinnamon	1/2 teaspoon ground nutmeg
1/4 teaspoon ground cloves	

Directions:

(1) Set the Zojirushi bread maker to the Quick Bread setting and preheat it. *(2)* Pumpkin puree,

shredded zucchini, eggs, vegetable oil, and vanilla essence should all be combined in a mixing dish. Blend thoroughly. *(3)* To make the flour, sugar, baking soda, baking powder, salt, nutmeg, cinnamon, and clove mixture, sift all of the ingredients in a separate bowl. *(4)* Gradually add the dry ingredients while stirring continuously once the wet ones have been well mixed. Make sure not to stir it too vigorously. *(5)* After adding the batter, cover the bread machine pan. *(6)* Choose the Quick Bread option and hit the start button. *(7)* Before serving, gently transfer the bread from the pan to a wire rack to cool. Once the cycle is done, slice it.

CHOCOLATE ZUCCHINI BREAD

Total Time: 3 hours 30 minutes | Prep Time: 20 minutes

Ingredients:

1 cup shredded zucchini	2 eggs
1/2 cup vegetable oil	1 teaspoon vanilla extract
1 1/4 cups all-purpose flour	1/2 cup unsweetened cocoa powder
1 cup granulated sugar	1 teaspoon baking soda
1/4 teaspoon baking powder	1/2 teaspoon salt
1 cup semisweet chocolate chips	

Directions:

(1) Set the Zojirushi bread maker to the Quick Bread setting and preheat it. *(2)* Shredded zucchini, eggs, vegetable oil, and vanilla essence should all be combined in a mixing dish. Blend thoroughly. *(3)* Coarsely mix the flour, sugar, baking powder, baking soda, and salt in an individual basin. *(4)* Stir until just blended, and gradually add the dry ingredients to the wet components. Take caution not to blend too much. *(5)* Add the chocolate chips and fold. *(6)* After adding the batter, cover the bread machine pan. *(7)* Choose the Quick Bread option and hit the start button. *(8)* After the cycle finishes, take the bread out of the pan and set it on a wire rack to cool. Prior to serving, cut it into slices.

APPLE ZUCCHINI BREAD

Total Time: 3 hours 15 minutes | Prep Time: 15 minutes

Ingredients:

1 cup shredded zucchini	1 cup peeled and grated apple
2 eggs	1/2 cup vegetable oil
1 teaspoon vanilla extract	1 1/2 cups all-purpose flour
1 cup granulated sugar	1 teaspoon baking soda
1/2 teaspoon baking powder	1/2 teaspoon salt
1 teaspoon ground cinnamon	1/2 teaspoon ground nutmeg
1/4 teaspoon ground cloves	

Directions:

(1) Set the Zojirushi bread maker to the Quick Bread setting and preheat it. *(2)* Shredded zucchini, grated apple, eggs, vegetable oil, and vanilla essence should all be combined in a mixing dish. Blend thoroughly. *(3)* Flour, sugar, baking soda, salt, nutmeg, cinnamon, and cloves should be sifted into a separate basin. *(4)* Stir until just blended, and gradually add the dry ingredients to the wet components. Take caution not to blend too much. *(5)* After adding the batter, cover the bread machine pan. *(6)* Choose the Quick Bread option and hit the start button. *(7)* After the cycle is finished, carefully move the bread to a wire rack to cool. Before serving, thinly slice it.

CRANBERRY ORANGE ZUCCHINI BREAD

Total Time: 3 hours 30 minutes | Prep Time: 20 minutes

Ingredients:

1 cup shredded zucchini	1/2 cup dried cranberries
Zest of 1 orange	2 eggs
1/2 cup vegetable oil	1 teaspoon vanilla extract
1 3/4 cups all-purpose flour	1 cup granulated sugar
1 teaspoon baking soda	1/2 teaspoon baking powder
1/2 teaspoon salt	1/2 cup orange juice

Directions:

(1) Set the Zojirushi bread maker to the Quick Bread setting and preheat it. *(2)* Orange zest and dried cranberries should be combined in a small basin. Put aside. *(3)* Shredded zucchini, eggs, vegetable oil, and vanilla essence should all be combined in a mixing dish. Blend thoroughly. *(4)* Transfer the flour, sugar, baking soda, baking powder, and salt to another basin and sift these ingredients. *(5)* Stirring until just blended, gradually add the dry ingredients to the liquid components, alternating with orange juice. Take caution not to blend too much. *(6)* Stir in the orange zest and cranberry mixture. *(7)* After adding the batter, cover the bread machine pan. *(8)* Choose the Quick Bread option and hit the start button. *(9)* Before slicing, the bread has to be gently taken out of the pan and let to cool on a wire rack. When the cycle is complete, it should be served.

MAPLE PECAN ZUCCHINI BREAD

Total Time: 3 hours | Prep Time: 20 minutes

Ingredients:

2 cups grated zucchini	3 large eggs
1 cup maple syrup	1/2 cup vegetable oil
1 teaspoon vanilla extract	2 cups all-purpose flour
1 teaspoon baking powder	1/2 teaspoon baking soda
1/2 teaspoon salt	1 teaspoon ground cinnamon
1/2 cup chopped pecans	

Directions:

(1) Set your Zojirushi bread maker to preheat. *(2)* Beat the eggs, oil, vanilla, and maple syrup thoroughly in a big basin. *(3)* Add the grated zucchini and stir. *(4)* Gather the dry Ingredients: flour, baking soda, baking powder, salt, and cinnamon. Set aside. *(5)* Mix until just incorporated, and gradually add the dry ingredients to the wet ones. *(6)* Add the chopped pecans and fold. *(7)* After adding the batter to the pan in the bread maker, choose the "Cake" or "Quick Bread" cycle. *(8)* As directed by the maker, turn on the machine and let it bake. *(9)* When the

bread is finished, take it out of the machine and allow it to cool before slicing.

ORANGE CRANBERRY ZUCCHINI BREAD

Total Time: 3 hours 30 minutes | Prep Time: 25 minutes

Ingredients:

2 cups grated zucchini	Zest of 1 orange
1/2 cup freshly squeezed orange juice	3/4 cup granulated sugar
1/2 cup vegetable oil	2 large eggs
2 cups all-purpose flour	1 teaspoon baking powder
1/2 teaspoon baking soda	1/2 teaspoon salt
1 cup dried cranberries	

Directions:

(1) Set your Zojirushi bread maker to preheat. *(2)* Grated zucchini, orange zest, orange juice, sugar, oil, and eggs should all be combined in a big basin. *(3)* Use a second bowl to combine the salt, baking soda, baking powder, and flour. *(4)* Mix until just incorporated, and gradually add the dry ingredients to the wet ones. *(5)* Add the dried cranberries and fold. *(6)* After adding the batter to the pan in the bread maker, choose the "Cake" or "Quick Bread" cycle. *(7)* As directed by the maker, turn on the machine and let it bake. *(8)* When the bread is finished, take it out of the machine and allow it to cool before slicing.

RASPBERRY ALMOND ZUCCHINI BREAD

Total Time: 3 hours 15 minutes | Prep Time: 30 minutes

Ingredients:

2 cups grated zucchini	1 cup fresh or frozen raspberries
1/2 cup sliced almonds	1/2 cup granulated sugar
1/2 cup brown sugar	1/2 cup vegetable oil
2 large eggs	2 teaspoons almond extract
2 cups all-purpose flour	1 teaspoon baking powder

1/2 teaspoon baking   1/2 teaspoon salt
soda

Directions:

(1) Set your Zojirushi bread maker to preheat. *(2)* Grated zucchini, raspberries, sliced almonds, sugars, oil, eggs, and almond essence should all be combined in a big dish. *(3)* Use a second bowl to combine the salt, baking soda, baking powder, and flour. *(4)* Mix until just incorporated, and gradually add the dry ingredients to the wet ones. *(5)* After adding the batter to the pan in the bread maker, choose the "Cake" or "Quick Bread" cycle. *(6)* As directed by the maker, turn on the machine and let it bake. *(7)* When the bread is finished, take it out of the machine and allow it to cool before slicing.

CINNAMON RAISIN ZUCCHINI BREAD

Total Time: 3 hours 10 minutes | Prep Time: 15 minutes

Ingredients:

2 cups grated zucchini	1 cup raisins
1/2 cup granulated sugar	1/2 cup brown sugar
1/2 cup vegetable oil	2 large eggs
2 teaspoons ground cinnamon	2 cups all-purpose flour
1 teaspoon baking powder	1/2 teaspoon baking soda
1/2 teaspoon salt	

Directions:

(1) Start the Zojirushi bread machine by preheating it. *(2)* Mix the grated zucchini, raisins, sugars, oil, eggs, and crushed cinnamon together in a large bowl. Blend until well combined. *(3)* Flour, baking soda, salt, baking powder, and baking powder should be whisked together in a separate basin. *(4)* Carefully combine the dry and wet components by mixing them slowly until they are nearly combined. *(5)* The batter should be poured into the pan of the bread machine, and then the "Quick Bread" or "Cake" cycle should be selected. *(6)* After starting the machine, wait for it to bake in accordance with the instructions provided by the manufacturer. *(7)* After the bread has finished baking, take it out of the machine and allow it to cool before slicing it.

LEMON POPPY SEED ZUCCHINI BREAD

Total Time: 3 hours 20 minutes | Prep Time: 20 minutes

Ingredients:

2 cups grated zucchini	Zest of 2 lemons
1/4 cup freshly squeezed lemon juice	1/2 cup granulated sugar
1/2 cup brown sugar	1/2 cup vegetable oil
2 large eggs	2 tablespoons poppy seeds
2 cups all-purpose flour	1 teaspoon baking powder
1/2 teaspoon baking soda	1/2 teaspoon salt

Directions:

(1) Set your Zojirushi bread maker to preheat. *(2)* Grated zucchini, lemon zest, lemon juice, sugars, oil, eggs, and poppy seeds should all be combined in a big basin. *(3)* The flour, baking soda, salt, and baking powder should be mixed separately. Combine just until blended, then add dry ingredients to wet one little at a time. *(4)* After adding the batter to the pan in the bread maker, choose the "Cake" or "Quick Bread" cycle. *(5)* As directed by the maker, turn on the machine and let it bake. *(6)* When the bread is finished, take it out of the machine and allow it to cool before slicing.

GINGERBREAD ZUCCHINI BREAD

Total Time: 3 hours | Prep Time: 15 minutes

Ingredients:

2 cups shredded zucchini	3 eggs
1 cup brown sugar	1/2 cup vegetable oil
1/4 cup molasses	2 teaspoons vanilla extract
2 cups all-purpose flour	1 teaspoon baking soda
1/2 teaspoon baking powder	1 teaspoon ground cinnamon
1/2 teaspoon ground ginger	1/4 teaspoon ground nutmeg
1/4 teaspoon salt	1/2 cup chopped walnuts (optional)

Directions:

(1) Set your Zojirushi bread maker to preheat. *(2)* Throw everything into a large basin and mix in the shredded zucchini, eggs, molasses, vegetable oil, brown sugar, and vanilla essence. Mix until well combined. *(3)* Put the flour, baking soda, nutmeg, cinnamon, and ginger into a separate bowl and sift them together. *(4)* Stir until just blended, and gradually add the dry ingredients to the wet components. If desired, fold in chopped walnuts. *(5)* Transfer the mixture to the pan of the bread maker. *(6)* On your bread machine, select "Cake" or "Quick Bread" and hit "Start." *(7)* Slice the bread when it has cooled on a wire rack, taking care to remove it from the machine after the cycle is complete.

CHAI SPICE ZUCCHINI BREAD

Total Time: 3 hours | Prep Time: 15 minutes

Ingredients:

2 cups shredded zucchini	3 eggs
1 cup granulated sugar	1/2 cup vegetable oil
1/4 cup honey	2 teaspoons vanilla extract
2 cups all-purpose flour	1 teaspoon baking soda
1/2 teaspoon baking powder	1 teaspoon ground cinnamon
1/2 teaspoon ground cardamom	1/2 teaspoon ground ginger
1/4 teaspoon ground cloves	1/4 teaspoon ground black pepper
1/4 teaspoon salt	1/2 cup chopped pecans (optional)

Directions:

(1) Set your Zojirushi bread maker to preheat. *(2)* Make sure to mix the shredded zucchini, eggs, sugar, vegetable oil, honey, and vanilla essence in a large basin. Mix until smooth. *(3)* Sift flour, baking powder, baking soda, cloves, ginger, cinnamon, cardamom, black pepper, and salt in a separate basin. *(4)* Stir until just blended, and gradually add the dry ingredients to the wet components. If desired, fold in chopped pecans. *(5)* Transfer the mixture to the pan of the bread maker. *(6)* On your bread machine, select "Cake" or "Quick Bread" and hit "Start." *(7)* With caution,

remove the bread from the machine once the cycle ends and place it on a wire rack to cool before slicing.

WALNUT ZUCCHINI BREAD

Total Time: 3 hours | Prep Time: 15 minutes

Ingredients:

2 cups shredded zucchini	3 eggs
1 cup granulated sugar	1/2 cup vegetable oil
1 teaspoon almond extract	2 cups all-purpose flour
1 teaspoon baking soda	1/2 teaspoon baking powder
1/2 teaspoon salt	1 teaspoon ground cinnamon
1/2 cup chopped walnuts	

Directions:

(1) Set your Zojirushi bread maker to preheat. *(2)* Shredded zucchini, eggs, sugar, vegetable oil, and almond essence should all be combined in a big basin. Blend thoroughly. *(3)* Flour, baking soda, salt, cinnamon, and baking powder should all be mixed in their own bowl. *(4)* Stir until just blended, and gradually add the dry ingredients to the wet components. Add the chopped walnuts and fold. *(5)* Transfer the mixture to the pan of the bread maker. *(6)* On your bread machine, select "Cake" or "Quick Bread" and hit "Start." *(7)* After the cycle is complete, carefully remove the bread from the machine and place it on a wire rack to cool. Then, slice it.

BLUEBERRY ZUCCHINI BREAD

Total Time: 3 hours | Prep Time: 15 minutes

Ingredients:

2 cups shredded zucchini	3 eggs
1 cup granulated sugar	1/2 cup vegetable oil
2 teaspoons lemon zest	2 teaspoons vanilla extract
2 cups all-purpose flour	1 teaspoon baking soda
1/2 teaspoon baking powder	1/4 teaspoon salt

1 cup fresh
blueberries

Directions:

(1) Set your Zojirushi bread maker to preheat. **(2)** Shredded zucchini, eggs, sugar, vegetable oil, lemon zest, and vanilla extract should all be combined in a big basin. Blend thoroughly. **(3)** The flour, baking soda, salt, and baking powder should be sifted into separate bowls. **(4)** Stir until just blended, and gradually add the dry ingredients to the wet components. Fold in the fresh blueberries gently. **(5)** Transfer the mixture to the pan of the bread maker. **(6)** On your bread machine, select "Cake" or "Quick Bread" and hit "Start." **(7)** Carefully remove the bread from the machine once the cycle is complete, and set it on a wire rack to cool before slicing.

STRAWBERRY ZUCCHINI BREAD

Total Time: 3 hours | Prep Time: 15 minutes

Ingredients:

2 cups shredded zucchini	3 eggs
1 cup granulated sugar	1/2 cup vegetable oil
1/4 cup milk	2 teaspoons vanilla extract
2 cups all-purpose flour	1 teaspoon baking soda
1/2 teaspoon baking powder	1/4 teaspoon salt
1 cup chopped fresh strawberries	

Directions:

(1) Set your Zojirushi bread maker to preheat. **(2)** Gather all the ingredients in a large basin: shredded zucchini, eggs, sugar, milk, vegetable oil, and vanilla essence. Mix until well combined. **(3)** Make a second bowl to sift the flour, baking soda, salt, and baking powder. **(4)** Stir until just blended, and gradually add the dry ingredients to the wet components. Add the diced fresh strawberries and fold gently. **(5)** Transfer the mixture to the pan of the bread maker. **(6)** On your bread machine, select "Cake" or "Quick Bread" and hit "Start." **(7)** Carefully remove the bread from the machine once the cycle is complete, and set it on a wire rack to cool before slicing.

RASPBERRY ZUCCHINI BREAD

Total Time: 3 hours 30 minutes | Prep Time: 15 minutes | Yield: 1 loaf

Ingredients:

1 cup shredded zucchini	1/2 cup fresh raspberries
2 eggs	1/2 cup vegetable oil
1 teaspoon vanilla extract	1 1/2 cups all-purpose flour
1/2 cup granulated sugar	1/2 teaspoon baking powder
1/2 teaspoon baking soda	1/2 teaspoon salt
1 teaspoon ground cinnamon	

Directions:

(1) Set your Zojirushi bread maker to preheat. **(2)** Oil and dust a 9 x 5-inch loaf pan. **(3)** In a large basin, mix together the raspberries, eggs, zucchini shreds, vegetable oil, and vanilla extract. Mix until smooth. **(4)** After that, take a separate dish and sift the cinnamon, sugar, baking soda, baking powder, salt, and flour. **(5)** Stir until just blended, and gradually add the dry ingredients to the wet components. **(6)** After the loaf pan is ready, pour the batter into it. **(7)** After inserting the loaf pan into the bread maker, choose the "Quick Bread" option. **(8)** Once the machine has started, let it do its thing. **(9)** After the bread has finished baking, carefully take it out of the machine and allow it to cool for ten minutes in the pan. **(10)** Before slicing and serving, move the bread to a wire rack to cool fully.

BLACKBERRY ZUCCHINI BREAD

Total Time: 3 hours | Prep Time: 15 minutes

Ingredients:

1 cup grated zucchini	1/2 cup fresh blackberries
2 eggs	1/2 cup vegetable oil
1 cup granulated sugar	1 teaspoon vanilla extract
2 cups all-purpose flour	1 teaspoon baking powder
1/2 teaspoon baking soda	1/2 teaspoon salt

1 teaspoon ground cinnamon	1/2 teaspoon ground nutmeg

Directions:

(1) Preheat your Zojirushi bread maker in accordance with the manufacturer's guidelines. **(2)** A big basin is the best place to combine the grated zucchini, blackberries, eggs, vegetable oil, sugar, and vanilla aromatic extract. Mix until smooth. **(3)** The flour, baking soda, nutmeg, cinnamon, baking powder, and salt should all be combined in a separate basin. **(4)** Stir until just blended, and gradually add the dry ingredients to the wet components. Avoid over-mixing. **(5)** Transfer the mixture to the bread pan in the bread maker. **(6)** On your Zojirushi bread maker, select "Quick Bread" and set the timer for three hours. **(7)** After the baking cycle has finished, take the bread pan out of the machine with care, letting it cool before slicing and serving.

PEACH ZUCCHINI BREAD

Total Time: 3 hours 30 minutes | Prep Time: 15 minutes | Yield: 1 loaf

Ingredients:

1 medium zucchini, grated (about 1 cup)	2 ripe peaches, peeled and diced
2 cups all-purpose flour	1 teaspoon baking powder
1/2 teaspoon baking soda	1/2 teaspoon salt
1 teaspoon ground cinnamon	1/2 teaspoon ground nutmeg
2 large eggs	1/2 cup granulated sugar
1/2 cup brown sugar	1/2 cup vegetable oil
1 teaspoon vanilla extract	

Directions:

(1) Start your Zojirushi bread machine on "Quick Bread" and lightly grease the pan. **(2)** Mix grated zucchini and diced peaches in a medium bowl. Set aside. **(3)** A big basin is the best place to mix the dry Ingredients: flour, baking soda, salt, cinnamon, and nutmeg. **(4)** Beat eggs with granulated and brown sugar in another dish until creamy. **(5)** Slowly add vegetable oil and vanilla to the egg mixture and whisk. **(6)** Gradually combine the dry and wet components.

(7) Spread zucchini and peaches evenly in batter. **(8)** Fill your Zojirushi bread machine pan with batter. **(9)** Close the lid and select "Quick Bread." Feel free to alter the crust. **(10)** To activate the bread maker, simply press the start button. After the pan has cooled for 10 minutes, remove it from the machine and set it on a wire rack to cool completely. **(11)** Peach Zucchini Bread is delicious alone or with whipped cream or butter. Enjoy!

APRICOT ZUCCHINI BREAD

Total Time: 3 hours 30 minutes | Prep Time: 20 minutes | Yield: 1 loaf

Ingredients:

1 cup grated zucchini	1/2 cup dried apricots, chopped
2 eggs	1/2 cup vegetable oil
1 cup granulated sugar	1 teaspoon vanilla extract
2 cups all-purpose flour	1 teaspoon baking powder
1/2 teaspoon baking soda	1/2 teaspoon salt
1 teaspoon ground cinnamon	1/2 teaspoon ground nutmeg
1/4 cup chopped walnuts (optional)	

Directions:

(1) As directed by the manufacturer, preheat your Zojirushi bread maker using the quick bread setting. **(2)** A large basin is ideal for combining the following Ingredients: grated zucchini, chopped apricots, eggs, vegetable oil, sugar, and vanilla essence. Mix until smooth. **(3)** With nutmeg, cinnamon, salt, baking soda, and powder in one dish, sift the flour and baking ingredients into another. **(4)** Stir until just blended, and gradually add the dry ingredients to the wet components. Take caution not to blend too much. **(5)** Stir in the chopped walnuts if using. **(6)** Fill the bread pan of your Zojirushi bread maker with the batter. **(7)** Shut the cover and choose the quick bread option. **(8)** The bread machine will mix, knead, and bake the bread if you press the start button. **(9)** Carefully remove the bread from the pan when the cycle is ended and set it on a wire rack to cool before slicing.

FIG ZUCCHINI BREAD

Total Time: 3 hours 30 minutes | Prep Time: 20 minutes | Yield: 1 loaf

Ingredients:

1 cup grated zucchini	1/2 cup dried figs, chopped
2 eggs	1/2 cup vegetable oil
1 cup granulated sugar	1 teaspoon vanilla extract
2 cups all-purpose flour	1 teaspoon baking powder
1/2 teaspoon baking soda	1/2 teaspoon salt
1 teaspoon ground cinnamon	1/2 teaspoon ground nutmeg
1/4 cup chopped almonds (optional)	

Directions:

(1) Use the quick bread setting to preheat your Zojirushi bread maker in accordance with the manufacturer's instructions. *(2)* Shred the zucchini and add it to a big basin with the sliced figs, eggs, vegetable oil, sugar, and vanilla essence. Mix well. Give it a good stir. *(3)* Next, mix the flour, baking soda, salt, cinnamon, nutmeg, and nutmeg in a separate basin. *(4)* Stir the dry ingredients until they are barely incorporated before gradually adding them to the wet components. Don't mix too much at once. *(5)* Add the chopped almonds and mix, if using. *(6)* Fill the Zojirushi bread machine's bread pan with the batter. *(7)* Once the lid is closed, choose the fast bread setting. *(8)* To begin mixing, kneading, and baking the bread, press the start button. *(9)* After the cooking cycle is over, carefully transfer the bread to a cooling rack made of wire. Once cold, proceed to slice.

DATE ZUCCHINI BREAD

Total Time: 3 hours | Prep Time: 15 minutes

Ingredients:

1 cup shredded zucchini	1/2 cup chopped dates
1/2 cup chopped walnuts	2 cups all-purpose flour
1 teaspoon baking powder	1/2 teaspoon baking soda
1/2 teaspoon salt	1 teaspoon ground cinnamon
1/2 teaspoon ground nutmeg	2 large eggs
1/2 cup vegetable oil	1/2 cup granulated sugar
1/2 cup brown sugar	1 teaspoon vanilla extract

Directions:

(1) Set your Zojirushi bread maker to preheat. *(2)* Combine the chopped walnuts, chopped dates, and shredded zucchini in a big basin. Put aside. *(3)* Toss the cinnamon, nutmeg, salt, baking soda, baking powder, and flour in a separate bowl. *(4)* Separate bowl for whirling the eggs. Combine the oil, brown sugar, granulated sugar, and vanilla essence. Combine well. *(5)* Mix until just incorporated, and gradually add the dry ingredients to the wet ones. *(6)* In order to spread the zucchini, date, and walnut combination evenly, fold them in. *(7)* After adding the batter to the pan, choose "Quick Bread" or "Cake" on the bread machine. *(8)* Start the machine and set the timer for two hours. *(9)* When the baking process is finished, take the bread out of the pan with care and let it cool on a wire rack before slicing and serving.

PLUM ZUCCHINI BREAD

Total Time: 3 hours 30 minutes | Prep Time: 20 minutes

Ingredients:

1 cup shredded zucchini	1 cup diced plums
1/2 cup chopped pecans	2 cups all-purpose flour
1 teaspoon baking powder	1/2 teaspoon baking soda
1/2 teaspoon salt	1 teaspoon ground cinnamon
1/2 teaspoon ground ginger	2 large eggs
1/2 cup vegetable oil	1/2 cup granulated sugar
1/2 cup brown sugar	1 teaspoon vanilla extract

Directions:

(1) Set your Zojirushi bread maker to preheat. *(2)* Diced plums, chopped pecans, and shredded

zucchini should all be combined in a big basin. Put aside. *(3)* Measure and combine the flour, baking soda, baking powder, salt, ginger, cinnamon, and a separate dish. *(4)* Beat the eggs in another basin. Incorporate the vanilla essence, brown sugar, granulated sugar, and vegetable oil. Blend thoroughly. *(5)* Mix until just incorporated, and gradually add the dry ingredients to the wet ones. *(6)* In order to spread the zucchini, plum, and pecan mixture evenly, fold them in. *(7)* After adding the batter to the pan, choose "Quick Bread" or "Cake" on the bread machine. *(8)* Start the machine and set the timer for two hours and thirty minutes. *(9)* When the baking process is finished, take the bread out of the pan with care and let it cool on a wire rack before slicing and serving.

CHERRY ZUCCHINI BREAD

Total Time: 3 hours 15 minutes | Prep Time: 25 minutes

Ingredients:

1 cup shredded zucchini	1 cup chopped cherries (fresh or frozen)
1/2 cup sliced almonds	2 cups all-purpose flour
1 teaspoon baking powder	1/2 teaspoon baking soda
1/2 teaspoon salt	1 teaspoon ground cinnamon
1/2 teaspoon almond extract	2 large eggs
1/2 cup vegetable oil	1/2 cup granulated sugar
1/2 cup brown sugar	

Directions:

(1) Set your Zojirushi bread maker to preheat. *(2)* Sliced almonds, chopped cherries, and zucchini shreds should all be combined in a big basin. Put aside. *(3)* Gather the dry Ingredients: flour, baking soda, baking powder, salt, and cinnamon. Set aside. *(4)* Beat the eggs in another basin. Incorporate the almond extract, brown sugar, granulated sugar, and vegetable oil. Blend thoroughly. *(5)* Mix until just incorporated, and gradually add the dry ingredients to the wet ones. *(6)* Once uniformly distributed, fold in the zucchini, cherry, and almond mixture. *(7)* After

adding the batter to the pan, choose "Quick Bread" or "Cake" on the bread machine. *(8)* Start the machine and set the timer for three hours and fifteen minutes. *(9)* When the baking process is finished, take the bread out of the pan with care and let it cool on a wire rack before slicing and serving.

PISTACHIO ZUCCHINI BREAD

Total Time: 3 hours 30 minutes | Prep Time: 20 minutes

Ingredients:

1 cup shredded zucchini	1/2 cup chopped pistachios
1/2 cup raisins	2 cups all-purpose flour
1 teaspoon baking powder	1/2 teaspoon baking soda
1/2 teaspoon salt	1 teaspoon ground cinnamon
1/2 teaspoon ground cardamom	2 large eggs
1/2 cup vegetable oil	1/2 cup granulated sugar
1/2 cup brown sugar	1 teaspoon vanilla extract

Directions:

(1) Set your Zojirushi bread maker to preheat. *(2)* Combine the raisins, chopped pistachios, and zucchini shreds in a big basin. Put aside. *(3)* In an independent basin, combine the flour, baking powder, baking soda, salt, cinnamon, and cardamom. *(4)* Beat the eggs in another basin. Incorporate the vanilla essence, brown sugar, granulated sugar, and vegetable oil. Blend thoroughly. *(5)* Mix until just incorporated, and gradually add the dry ingredients to the wet ones. *(6)* In order to spread the zucchini, pistachio, and raisin combination evenly, fold them in. *(7)* After adding the batter to the pan, choose "Quick Bread" or "Cake" on the bread machine. *(8)* Start the machine and set the timer for three hours and thirty minutes. *(9)* When the baking process is finished, take the bread out of the pan with care and let it cool on a wire rack before slicing and serving.

HAZELNUT ZUCCHINI BREAD

Total Time: 3 hours 15 minutes | Prep Time: 25 minutes

Ingredients:

1 cup shredded zucchini	1/2 cup chopped hazelnuts
1/2 cup chocolate chips	2 cups all-purpose flour
1 teaspoon baking powder	1/2 teaspoon baking soda
1/2 teaspoon salt	1 teaspoon ground cinnamon
1/2 teaspoon ground nutmeg	2 large eggs
1/2 cup vegetable oil	1/2 cup granulated sugar
1/2 cup brown sugar	1 teaspoon vanilla extract

Directions:

(1) Set your Zojirushi bread maker to preheat. *(2)* Combine the chocolate chips, chopped hazelnuts, and shredded zucchini in a big basin. Put aside. *(3)* In another dish, combine the flour, baking soda, baking powder, salt, cinnamon, and nutmeg. *(4)* Beat the eggs in another basin. Incorporate the vanilla essence, brown sugar, granulated sugar, and vegetable oil. Blend thoroughly. *(5)* Mix until just incorporated, and gradually add the dry ingredients to the wet ones. *(6)* Stir in the chocolate chip, hazelnut, and zucchini mixture until well combined. *(7)* After adding the batter to the pan, choose "Quick Bread" or "Cake" on the bread machine. *(8)* Start the machine and set the timer for three hours and fifteen minutes. *(9)* When the baking process is finished, take the bread out of the pan with care and let it cool on a wire rack before slicing and serving.

PECAN ZUCCHINI BREAD

Total Time: 3 hours 30 minutes | Prep Time: 15 minutes | Yield: 1 loaf

Ingredients:

2 cups shredded zucchini	3 eggs
1 cup vegetable oil	2 cups granulated sugar
3 teaspoons vanilla extract	3 cups all-purpose flour
1 teaspoon baking powder	1/4 teaspoon baking soda
1 teaspoon salt	1 tablespoon ground cinnamon
1 cup chopped pecans	

Directions:

(1) Set the "Quick Bread" setting on your Zojirushi bread maker to preheat. *(2)* A big mixing bowl is the perfect place to combine the shredded zucchini, eggs, sugar, vegetable oil, and vanilla essence. Combine well. *(3)* Second, in another dish, mix together the dry Ingredients: cinnamon, salt, baking powder, baking soda, and flour. *(4)* Mix until just incorporated, and gradually add the dry ingredients to the wet ones. Add chopped pecans and stir. *(5)* Fill the bread pan of your bread maker with the batter. *(6)* Shut the cover and choose the "Quick Bread" option. Adjust the crust to your preferred thickness. *(7)* The bread maker is as easy as turning it on and leaving it to bake. Once the cycle finishes, carefully take the loaf out of the pan and set it on a wire rack to cool. Slice it afterward.

COCONUT ZUCCHINI BREAD

Total Time: 3 hours 30 minutes | Prep Time: 15 minutes | Yield: 1 loaf

Ingredients:

2 cups shredded zucchini	3 eggs
1 cup vegetable oil	1 1/2 cups granulated sugar
1 tablespoon vanilla extract	2 cups all-purpose flour
1 teaspoon baking powder	1/2 teaspoon baking soda
1/2 teaspoon salt	1 teaspoon ground cinnamon
1 cup shredded coconut	

Directions:

(1) Set the "Quick Bread" setting on your Zojirushi bread maker to preheat. *(2)* Gather all the ingredients in a big bowl: shredded zucchini, eggs, sugar, vegetable oil, and vanilla essence. Mix all ingredients together. *(3)* Toss the cinnamon, baking soda, salt, baking powder, and

flour into a separate dish. *(4)* Stir until just blended, and gradually add the dry ingredients to the wet components. Add the coconut shreds and fold. *(5)* Fill the bread pan of your bread maker with the batter. *(6)* Shut the cover and choose the "Quick Bread" option. Select the crust setting that you like most. *(7)* To begin baking, press the start button on the bread maker. When finished, carefully remove the loaf and allow it to cool before slicing.

HONEY ZUCCHINI BREAD

Total Time: 3 hours | Prep Time: 20 minutes

Ingredients:

1 cup shredded zucchini	2 eggs
1/2 cup honey	1/2 cup vegetable oil
1 teaspoon vanilla extract	1 3/4 cups all-purpose flour
1 teaspoon baking powder	1/2 teaspoon baking soda
1/2 teaspoon salt	1 teaspoon ground cinnamon

Directions:

(1) Follow the manufacturer's instructions to preheat the Zojirushi bread machine. *(2)* The eggs should be beaten in a big basin. Combine the zucchini shreds, honey, oil from vegetables, and vanilla essence by stirring thoroughly. *(3)* Combine the cinnamon, salt, baking soda, flour, and baking powder in a separate basin. *(4)* While whisking constantly, slowly incorporate the dry ingredients into the wet mixture. *(5)* Before sealing the bread machine top, pour the batter into the pan. *(6)* The bread machine's "Quick Bread" preset can be accessed by pressing the start button. *(7)* Carefully take the bread out of the machine when it's done baking and set it aside to cool before cutting and serving.

MAPLE ZUCCHINI BREAD

Total Time: 3 hours 15 minutes | Prep Time: 25 minutes

Ingredients:

1 cup shredded zucchini	2 eggs
1/2 cup pure maple syrup	1/2 cup vegetable oil
1 teaspoon vanilla extract	1 3/4 cups all-purpose flour
1 teaspoon baking powder	1/2 teaspoon baking soda
1/2 teaspoon salt	1 teaspoon ground cinnamon

Directions:

(1) Follow the manufacturer's instructions to preheat the Zojirushi bread machine. *(2)* The eggs should be beaten in a big basin. Mash the shredded zucchini with the maple syrup, oil from vegetables, and vanilla essence until everything is incorporated. *(3)* Combine the cinnamon, salt, baking soda, flour, and baking powder in a separate basin. *(4)* While whisking constantly, slowly incorporate the dry ingredients into the wet mixture. *(5)* Before sealing the bread machine top, pour the batter into the pan. *(6)* The bread machine's "Quick Bread" preset can be accessed by pressing the start button. *(7)* Carefully take the bread out of the machine when it's done baking and set it aside to cool before cutting and serving.

BROWN SUGAR ZUCCHINI BREAD

Total Time: 3 hours 30 minutes | Prep Time: 30 minutes

Ingredients:

1 cup shredded zucchini	2 eggs
3/4 cup packed brown sugar	1/2 cup vegetable oil
1 teaspoon vanilla extract	1 3/4 cups all-purpose flour
1 teaspoon baking powder	1/2 teaspoon baking soda
1/2 teaspoon salt	1 teaspoon ground cinnamon

Directions:

(1) Follow the manufacturer's instructions to preheat the Zojirushi bread machine. *(2)* The eggs should be beaten in a big basin. Brown sugar, vegetable oil, shredded zucchini, and vanilla essence should all be mixed together. *(3)* Combine the cinnamon, salt, baking soda, flour, and baking powder in a separate basin. *(4)* While whisking constantly, slowly incorporate the dry

ingredients into the wet mixture. *(5)* Before sealing the bread machine top, pour the batter into the pan. *(6)* The bread machine's "Quick Bread" preset can be accessed by pressing the start button. *(7)* Carefully take the bread out of the machine when it's done baking and set it aside to cool before cutting and serving.

CINNAMON ZUCCHINI BREAD

Total Time: 3 hours | Prep Time: 15 minutes

Ingredients:

1 cup shredded zucchini, excess moisture squeezed out	2 large eggs
1/2 cup vegetable oil	1 cup granulated sugar
1 teaspoon vanilla extract	1 3/4 cups all-purpose flour
1 teaspoon baking powder	1/2 teaspoon baking soda
1/2 teaspoon salt	2 teaspoons ground cinnamon
1/2 cup chopped walnuts (optional)	

Directions:

(1) Zojirushi bread machine preheat. *(2)* Beat eggs, vegetable oil, sugar, and vanilla essence in a large bowl. *(3)* Before mixing the dry components with the wet ones, shred the zucchini. *(4)* It is imperative that the dry components be separated into separate basins. These components include flour, baking soda, cinnamon powder, baking powder, and salt. *(5)* Toss the dry ingredients with the liquid ones and stir until just combined. Whisk gently. *(6)* Fold in chopped walnuts if using. *(7)* Pour batter into your Zojirushi bread machine's greased pan. *(8)* Set your machine's crust to "Quick Bread" and customize it. *(9)* Start the machine with the lid closed. *(10)* Carefully remove the bread from the machine after baking and let it cool on a wire rack. Slice and serve. Munch on some Cinnamon Zucchini Bread!

NUTELLA ZUCCHINI BREAD

Total Time: 3 hours 15 minutes | Prep Time: 20 minutes

Ingredients:

1 cup shredded zucchini, excess moisture squeezed out	2 large eggs
1/2 cup vegetable oil	1 cup granulated sugar
1 teaspoon vanilla extract	1 3/4 cups all-purpose flour
1 teaspoon baking powder	1/2 teaspoon baking soda
1/2 teaspoon salt	1/2 cup Nutella (or other hazelnut spread)

Directions:

(1) Zojirushi bread machine preheat. *(2)* Beat eggs, vegetable oil, sugar, and vanilla essence in a large bowl. *(3)* Add shredded zucchini to wet ingredients and stir well. *(4)* Sift flour, baking powder, soda, and salt in another basin. *(5)* Toss will thoroughly combine the dry ingredients with the wet ingredients. *(6)* Gently mix Nutella into the batter to marble it. *(7)* Pour batter into your Zojirushi bread machine's greased pan. *(8)* Set your machine's crust to "Quick Bread" and customize it. *(9)* Start the machine with the lid closed. *(10)* Before slicing and serving, remove the bread from the oven with caution and let it cool on a wire rack. I like your zucchini bread with Nutella!

PEANUT BUTTER ZUCCHINI BREAD

Total Time: 3 hours 30 minutes | Prep Time: 25 minutes

Ingredients:

1 cup shredded zucchini, excess moisture squeezed out	2 large eggs
1/2 cup vegetable oil	1 cup granulated sugar
1 teaspoon vanilla extract	1 3/4 cups all-purpose flour
1 teaspoon baking powder	1/2 teaspoon baking soda
1/2 teaspoon salt	1/2 cup creamy peanut butter

Directions:

(1) Set your Zojirushi bread maker to preheat. (2) Beat the eggs, vegetable oil, sugar, and vanilla extract together thoroughly in a sizable basin. (3) Mix well after adding the shredded zucchini to the wet components. (4) With a separate bowl, sift the flour, baking soda, baking powder, and salt. (5) While the wet components are being blended, slowly add the dry ingredients and stir just till combined. Creamy peanut butter should be added to the batter and gently mixed together until evenly distributed. (6) If using a Zojirushi bread maker, oil the bread pan and pour batter into it. (7) To make a crust of any thickness, just set the machine to "Quick Bread" mode and bake as directed. (8) Please activate the gadget once you have turned off the cover. (9) To make the bread easier to slice and serve, remove it from the oven and set it on a wire rack to cool. This bread with peanut butter and zucchini will blow your taste buds away.

MARSHMALLOW ZUCCHINI BREAD

Total Time: 3 hours 45 minutes | Prep Time: 30 minutes

Ingredients:

1 cup shredded zucchini, excess moisture squeezed out	2 large eggs
1/2 cup vegetable oil	1 cup granulated sugar
1 teaspoon vanilla extract	1 3/4 cups all-purpose flour
1 teaspoon baking powder	1/2 teaspoon baking soda
1/2 teaspoon salt	1 cup miniature marshmallows

Directions:

(1) Set your Zojirushi bread maker to preheat. (2) Beat the eggs, vegetable oil, sugar, and vanilla extract together thoroughly in a sizable basin. (3) Mix well after adding the shredded zucchini to the wet components. (4) With a separate bowl, sift the flour, baking soda, baking powder, and salt. (5) Mix until incorporated, and gradually incorporate the dry ingredients into the wet ones. (6) Mildly fold in the little marshmallows until they are incorporated into the batter. (7) If

using a Zojirushi bread maker, oil the bread pan and pour batter into it. (8) Choose your machine's "Quick Bread" mode and adjust the crust to your desired thickness. (9) Shut off the cover and turn on the device. (10) After baking, let the bread rest entirely on a wire rack before slicing and serving. Top it all off with some Marshmallow Zucchini Bread and savor the delicious journey!

CREAM CHEESE ZUCCHINI BREAD

Total Time: 4 hours | Prep Time: 35 minutes

Ingredients:

1 cup shredded zucchini, excess moisture squeezed out	2 large eggs
1/2 cup vegetable oil	1 cup granulated sugar
1 teaspoon vanilla extract	1 3/4 cups all-purpose flour
1 teaspoon baking powder	1/2 teaspoon baking soda
1/2 teaspoon salt	4 ounces cream cheese, softened
1/4 cup powdered sugar	

Directions:

(1) Set your Zojirushi bread maker to preheat. (2) Beat the eggs, vegetable oil, sugar, and vanilla extract together thoroughly in a sizable basin. (3) Mix well after adding the shredded zucchini to the wet components. (4) With a separate bowl, sift the flour, baking soda, baking powder, and salt. (5) Mix until just incorporated, and gradually add the dry ingredients to the wet ones. (6) Beat the powdered sugar and softened cream cheese together until smooth in a separate bowl. (7) Till the cream cheese mixture is distributed evenly, gently fold it into the batter. (8) Grease the bread pan of your Zojirushi bread machine and pour the batter into it. (9) Choose your machine's "Quick Bread" mode and adjust the crust to your desired thickness. (10) Shut off the cover and turn on the device. (11) Remove the bread from the oven gently and let it rest on a wire rack. You may then slice it and serve it. This zucchini bread with cream cheese is delicious.

BUTTERSCOTCH ZUCCHINI BREAD

Total Time: 3 hours | Prep Time: 20 minutes

Ingredients:

2 cups shredded zucchini	3 eggs
1 cup granulated sugar	1 cup vegetable oil
1 teaspoon vanilla extract	3 cups all-purpose flour
1 teaspoon baking powder	1/2 teaspoon baking soda
1/2 teaspoon salt	1 cup butterscotch chips

Directions:

(1) Set your Zojirushi bread maker to preheat. *(2)* Beat the eggs in a big bowl until they are foamy. Mix in the oil, sugar, and vanilla essence. Blend thoroughly. *(3)* Add the zucchini shreds and stir. *(4)* Use a second bowl to combine the salt, baking soda, baking powder, and flour. *(5)* Stir until just blended, and gradually add the dry ingredients to the wet mixture. *(6)* Add the butterscotch chips and mix. *(7)* Fill the Zojirushi bread machine's bread pan with the batter. *(8)* Choose the "Quick Bread" option and hit the start button. *(9)* To cool the bread before slicing and serving, place it on a wire rack after taking it out of the oven.

CARAMEL ZUCCHINI BREAD

Total Time: 3 hours 15 minutes | Prep Time: 25 minutes

Ingredients:

2 cups shredded zucchini	3 eggs
1 cup brown sugar	1/2 cup white sugar
1/2 cup vegetable oil	1 teaspoon vanilla extract
3 cups all-purpose flour	1 teaspoon baking powder
1/2 teaspoon baking soda	1/2 teaspoon salt
1/2 cup caramel chips	

Directions:

(1) Set your Zojirushi bread maker to preheat. *(2)* Beat the eggs in a big bowl until they are foamy. Stir in oil, vanilla essence, brown and white

sugars. Blend thoroughly. *(3)* Add the zucchini shreds and stir. *(4)* Use a second bowl to combine the salt, baking soda, baking powder, and flour. *(5)* Stir until just blended, and gradually add the dry ingredients to the wet mixture. *(6)* Stir in the chocolate chunks. *(7)* Fill the Zojirushi bread machine's bread pan with the batter. *(8)* Choose the "Quick Bread" option and hit the start button. *(9)* After baking, let the bread rest entirely on a wire rack before cutting and serving.

PUMPKIN SPICE ZUCCHINI BREAD

Total Time: 3 hours 30 minutes | Prep Time: 30 minutes

Ingredients:

2 cups shredded zucchini	3 eggs
1 1/2 cups granulated sugar	1/2 cup vegetable oil
1 can (15 ounces) pumpkin puree	1 teaspoon vanilla extract
3 cups all-purpose flour	1 teaspoon baking powder
1 teaspoon baking soda	1/2 teaspoon salt
2 teaspoons ground cinnamon	1/2 teaspoon ground nutmeg
1/2 teaspoon ground ginger	1/4 teaspoon ground cloves

Directions:

(1) Set your Zojirushi bread maker to preheat. *(2)* Beat the eggs in a big bowl until they are foamy. Mix in the oil, sugar, vanilla essence, and pure pumpkin. Blend thoroughly. *(3)* Add the zucchini shreds and stir. *(4)* Stir together the flour, nutmeg, cinnamon, baking powder, baking soda, and cloves in a separate basin. *(5)* Stir until just blended, and gradually add the dry ingredients to the wet mixture. *(6)* Fill the Zojirushi bread machine's bread pan with the batter. *(7)* Choose the "Quick Bread" option and hit the start button. *(8)* After the bread has finished cooking, carefully place it on a wire rack to cool. After that, slice it and enjoy!

LEMON ZUCCHINI BREAD

Total Time: 3 hours 10 minutes | Prep Time: 20 minutes

Ingredients:

2 cups shredded zucchini	3 eggs
1 cup granulated sugar	1/2 cup vegetable oil
Zest of 2 lemons	Juice of 1 lemon
1 teaspoon vanilla extract	3 cups all-purpose flour
1 teaspoon baking powder	1/2 teaspoon baking soda
1/2 teaspoon salt	1/2 cup chopped walnuts (optional)

Directions:

(1) Set your Zojirushi bread maker to preheat. *(2)* Beat the eggs in a big bowl until they are foamy. Mix in the oil, sugar, juice, zest, and extract from the lemon. Blend thoroughly. *(3)* Add the zucchini shreds and stir. *(4)* Use a second bowl to combine the salt, baking soda, baking powder, and flour. Stir until just blended, and gradually add the dry ingredients to the wet mixture. *(5)* If using, fold in the chopped walnuts. *(6)* Fill the Zojirushi bread machine's bread pan with the batter. *(7)* Choose the "Quick Bread" option and hit the start button. *(8)* Removing the bread from the oven is a delicate process; once cooled, set it on a wire rack to serve.

ORANGE ZUCCHINI BREAD

Total Time: 3 hours 15 minutes | Prep Time: 25 minutes

Ingredients:

2 cups shredded zucchini	3 eggs
1 cup granulated sugar	1/2 cup vegetable oil
Zest of 2 oranges	Juice of 1 orange
1 teaspoon vanilla extract	3 cups all-purpose flour
1 teaspoon baking powder	1/2 teaspoon baking soda
1/2 teaspoon salt	1/2 cup chopped pecans (optional)

Directions:

(1) Set your Zojirushi bread maker to preheat. *(2)* Beat the eggs in a big bowl until they are foamy. Mix in the oil, sugar, juice, zest, and vanilla essence. Blend thoroughly. *(3)* Add the zucchini shreds and stir. *(4)* Use a second bowl to combine the salt, baking soda, baking powder, and flour. *(5)* Stir until just blended, and gradually add the dry ingredients to the wet mixture. *(6)* If using, mix in the chopped pecans. *(7)* Fill the Zojirushi bread machine's bread pan with the batter. *(8)* Choose the "Quick Bread" option and hit the start button. *(9)* After baking, let the bread rest entirely on a wire rack before cutting and serving.

LIME ZUCCHINI BREAD

Total Time: 3 hours 30 minutes | Prep Time: 15 minutes | Yield: 1 loaf

Ingredients:

2 cups all-purpose flour	1 teaspoon baking powder
1/2 teaspoon baking soda	1/2 teaspoon salt
1/2 cup unsalted butter, melted	1 cup granulated sugar
2 large eggs	1/4 cup fresh lime juice
1 teaspoon lime zest	1 cup grated zucchini
1/2 cup chopped walnuts (optional)	

Directions:

(1) Set the "Quick Bread" setting on your Zojirushi bread maker to preheat. *(2)* Toss the salt, baking powder, baking soda, and flour together in a medium-sized basin. Beat the sugar and melted butter together thoroughly in a large, separate bowl. *(3)* One egg at a time, adding and beating thoroughly after each addition. *(4)* Next, combine the lime zest and juice and mix well. *(5)* Little by little, whisk in the flour mixture until combined with the liquids. *(6)* If using, mix in the chopped walnuts and the grated zucchini. *(7)* After adding the batter, cover the bread machine pan. *(8)* Choose the "Quick Bread" option and hit the start button. *(9)* Using a spatula, carefully transfer the baked bread to a wire rack to cool after the baking cycle is finished. Proceed by slicing it.

GRAPEFRUIT ZUCCHINI BREAD

Total Time: 3 hours | Prep Time: 20 minutes

Ingredients:

1 medium zucchini, grated (about 1 cup)	2 cups all-purpose flour
1 teaspoon baking powder	1/2 teaspoon baking soda
1/2 teaspoon salt	1/2 cup granulated sugar
1/2 cup brown sugar	2 eggs
1/2 cup vegetable oil	1/4 cup fresh grapefruit juice
1 tablespoon grapefruit zest	1 teaspoon vanilla extract

Directions:

(1) Zojirushi bread machine preheat. *(2)* Oil or non-stick spray the bread pan. *(3)* Utilize a clean dish towel to squeeze excess moisture from grated zucchini. *(4)* Toss the salt, baking soda, flour, and baking powder together in a large basin. *(5)* In a separate dish, beat the eggs, brown sugar, granulated sugar, vegetable oil, grapefruit zest, and vanilla essence until well combined. *(6)* Just combine the dry and wet components by stirring them together. In no uncertain terms, do not overmix. Grated zucchini should be uniformly distributed in the batter. *(7)* Pour batter into the oiled Zojirushi bread machine pan. *(8)* Select "Quick Bread" or "Cake" on your bread machine and set the timer for 3 hours. *(9)* After baking, carefully remove the bread pan from the machine and let it cool for 10 minutes before moving it to a wire rack to finish cooling. *(10)* Enjoy Grapefruit Zucchini Bread sliced and served!

CRANBERRY ZUCCHINI BREAD

Total Time: 3 hours | Prep Time: 15 minutes | Yield: 1 loaf

Ingredients:

1 cup shredded zucchini	1/2 cup dried cranberries
2 eggs	1/2 cup vegetable oil
1 teaspoon vanilla extract	1 cup granulated sugar
1 1/2 cups all-purpose flour	1/2 teaspoon baking powder
1/2 teaspoon baking soda	1/2 teaspoon salt
1 teaspoon ground cinnamon	

Directions:

(1) Set your Zojirushi bread maker to preheat. *(2)* Put the dried cranberries and the shredded zucchini in a basin. *(3)* Beat the eggs in a separate basin and mix in the sugar, vanilla essence, and vegetable oil. Blend thoroughly. *(4)* In several bowls, whisk together the flour, baking powder, baking soda, salt, and cinnamon. *(5)* Stir until just blended, and gradually add the dry ingredients to the wet components. *(6)* Stir in the cranberry and zucchini combination. *(7)* Transfer the mixture to the pan of the bread maker. *(8)* On your Zojirushi bread maker, choose "Cake" or "Quick Bread" and begin the cycle. *(9)* After the bread has finished baking, take it out of the machine and allow it to cool before slicing.

CHERRY ALMOND ZUCCHINI BREAD

Total Time: 3 hours 15 minutes | Prep Time: 20 minutes | Yield: 1 loaf

Ingredients:

1 cup shredded zucchini	1/2 cup chopped almonds
1/2 cup dried cherries	2 eggs
1/2 cup vegetable oil	1 teaspoon almond extract
1 cup granulated sugar	1 1/2 cups all-purpose flour
1/2 teaspoon baking powder	1/2 teaspoon baking soda
1/2 teaspoon salt	

Directions:

(1) Set your Zojirushi bread maker to preheat. *(2)* Combine the dried cherries, sliced almonds, and shredded zucchini in a bowl. *(3)* Beat the eggs in a separate basin and mix in the sugar, almond essence, and vegetable oil. Blend thoroughly. *(4)* Toss the salt, baking powder, baking soda, and flour together in a separate bowl. *(5)* Stir until just blended, and gradually add the dry ingredients to the wet components. *(6)* Stir in the cherry, almond, and zucchini combination. *(7)* Transfer the mixture to the pan of the bread maker. *(8)* On your Zojirushi bread maker, choose "Cake" or "Quick Bread" and begin the cycle. *(9)* After the bread has finished baking, take it out of the machine and allow it to cool before slicing.

BLUEBERRY LEMON ZUCCHINI BREAD

Total Time: 3 hours 30 minutes | Prep Time: 25 minutes | Yield: 1 loaf

Ingredients:

1 cup shredded zucchini	1/2 cup fresh blueberries
Zest of 1 lemon	2 eggs
1/2 cup vegetable oil	1 tablespoon lemon juice
1 cup granulated sugar	1 1/2 cups all-purpose flour
1/2 teaspoon baking powder	1/2 teaspoon baking soda
1/2 teaspoon salt	

Directions:

(1) Set your Zojirushi bread maker to preheat. **(2)** Shredded zucchini, fresh blueberries, and lemon zest should all be combined in a basin. **(3)** While the eggs are being beaten, combine the sugar, lemon juice, and vegetable oil in another bowl. Combine well. **(4)** Toss the salt, baking powder, baking soda, and flour together in a separate bowl. **(5)** Stir until just blended, and gradually add the dry ingredients to the wet components. **(6)** Stir in the blueberries, zucchini, and mixture of lemon zest. **(7)** Transfer the mixture to the pan of the bread maker. **(8)** On your Zojirushi bread maker, choose "Cake" or "Quick Bread" and begin the cycle. **(9)** After the bread has finished baking, take it out of the machine and allow it to cool before slicing.

RASPBERRY COCONUT ZUCCHINI BREAD

Total Time: 3 hours | Prep Time: 20 minutes

Ingredients:

1 1/2 cups shredded zucchini	1 cup raspberries
1/2 cup shredded coconut	2 cups all-purpose flour
1 teaspoon baking powder	1/2 teaspoon baking soda
1/2 teaspoon salt	1/2 cup granulated sugar
1/2 cup brown sugar	2 eggs

1/2 cup vegetable oil   1 teaspoon vanilla extract

Directions:

(1) Zojirushi bread machine preheat. **(2)** Mix shredded zucchini, raspberries, and coconut in a large basin. **(3)** Separate basin for mixing flour, baking soda, salt, and baking powder. **(4)** Transfer to a separate basin and mix together the eggs, brown sugar, granulated sugar, vegetable oil, and vanilla essence. **(5)** Stir the dry ingredients into the liquid ones until well combined. **(6)** Mix zucchini, raspberry, and coconut till uniformly distributed. **(7)** Place the batter in the bread machine pan and select "Quick Bread" or "Cake." **(8)** Keep the lid closed and let the machine function. **(9)** After the bread is finished, take it out of the machine with care and let it cool on a wire rack. Then, slice it and serve.

PEACH PECAN ZUCCHINI BREAD

Total Time: 3 hours 30 minutes | Prep Time: 30 minutes

Ingredients:

1 1/2 cups shredded zucchini	1 cup chopped peaches
1/2 cup chopped pecans	2 cups all-purpose flour
1 teaspoon baking powder	1/2 teaspoon baking soda
1/2 teaspoon salt	1/2 cup granulated sugar
1/2 cup brown sugar	2 eggs
1/2 cup vegetable oil	1 teaspoon vanilla extract

Directions:

(1) Set your Zojirushi bread maker to preheat. **(2)** Add the chopped peaches, chopped pecans, and shredded zucchini to a large mixing bowl. **(3)** Use a second bowl to combine the salt, baking soda, baking powder, and flour. Beat the eggs, brown sugar, granulated sugar, vegetable oil, and vanilla extract together thoroughly in another bowl. **(4)** Mix until just incorporated, and gradually add the dry ingredients to the wet ones. **(5)** In order to spread the zucchini, peach, and pecan mixture evenly, fold them in. **(6)** After adding the batter to the pan, choose "Quick

Bread" or "Cake" on the bread machine. *(7)* Shut the cover and allow the device to perform its magic. *(8)* Once the bread has cooled slightly, transfer it to a wire rack and allow it to finish cooling completely before slicing and serving.

APPLE CINNAMON ZUCCHINI BREAD

Total Time: 3 hours 15 minutes | Prep Time: 25 minutes

Ingredients:

1 1/2 cups shredded zucchini	1 cup diced apples
1 teaspoon ground cinnamon	2 cups all-purpose flour
1 teaspoon baking powder	1/2 teaspoon baking soda
1/2 teaspoon salt	1/2 cup granulated sugar
1/2 cup brown sugar	2 eggs
1/2 cup vegetable oil	1 teaspoon vanilla extract

Directions:

(1) Set your Zojirushi bread maker to preheat. *(2)* Add the chopped apples, ground cinnamon, and zucchini shreds to a large mixing bowl. *(3)* Use a second bowl to combine the salt, baking soda, baking powder, and flour. *(4)* Beat the eggs, brown sugar, granulated sugar, vegetable oil, and vanilla extract together thoroughly in another bowl. *(5)* Mix until just incorporated, and gradually add the dry ingredients to the wet ones. *(6)* In order to spread the zucchini, apple, and cinnamon mixture evenly, fold them in. *(7)* After adding the batter to the pan, choose "Quick Bread" or "Cake" on the bread machine. *(8)* Shut the cover and allow the device to perform its magic. *(9)* Before slicing and serving, carefully take the bread from the machine once it has finished baking and place it on a wire rack to cool.

CARAMELIZED ONION AND BACON BREAD

Total Time: 3 hours 30 minutes | Prep Time: 40 minutes

Ingredients:

1 cup caramelized onions	1/2 cup cooked bacon, crumbled
2 cups all-purpose flour	1 teaspoon baking powder
1/2 teaspoon baking soda	1/2 teaspoon salt
1/2 cup grated Parmesan cheese	1/2 cup chopped fresh herbs
2 eggs	1/2 cup vegetable oil
1 teaspoon garlic powder	

Directions:

(1) Set your Zojirushi bread maker to preheat. *(2)* Grated Parmesan cheese, chopped fresh herbs, caramelized onions, and crumbled bacon should all be combined in a big mixing dish. *(3)* Flour in one bowl and salt, baking soda, garlic powder, and baking powder in another. *(4)* Beat the eggs and vegetable oil together thoroughly in another bowl. *(5)* Mix until just incorporated, and gradually add the dry ingredients to the wet ones. *(6)* In order to spread the onion, bacon, and herb combination evenly, fold them in. *(7)* After adding the batter to the pan, choose "Quick Bread" or "Cake" on the bread machine. *(8)* Shut the cover and allow the device to perform its magic. *(9)* Handle the bread carefully after it is completed baking, and set it on a wire rack to cool completely before cutting and serving.

THE END

Made in United States
Cleveland, OH
12 February 2025

14312841R00052